For Jackie and Catherine

Contents

Acknowledgements

Several people have helped with the preparation of this book. I must especially thank Julian Ingram, who helped with some of the research, and Peter Knowlson, of the Liberal party's research department, who was unfailingly helpful throughout the book's preparation. Without Harry Treadwell's assistance I would probably not have started writing it at all.

David Steel, members of his family, friends and political colleagues have given very generously of their time for interviews for which I am exceptionally grateful. David Steel has kindly read the draft of the book for accuracy, but he has made no comments on the opinions expressed therein. These opinions are solely my responsibility, as are any errors or failings in the book.

Christine Donougher of W. H. Allen has been a most helpful editor. Finally, I must give a big thank you to my secretaries Teresa Wood and Sharon Corder for typing out the book and dealing with the many amendments and corrections with their usual efficiency and cheerfulness.

Peter Bartram
25 June 1981

Foreword

My allegiance to David Steel is on three levels. As a Liberal; he is my leader; as a resident of the Borders, he is my MP; and as a neighbour, he is my friend. The first time we met was while sharing the platform at the Liberal party conference at Scarborough in 1965. At that time I was on the point of leaving active Liberal politics, while he had just come into them. Since then I have watched with admiration and interest his progress from the back-bencher who so courageously and meticulously steered the abortion reform bill on to the statute book, to his present position as party leader.

I have also watched him nearer at hand. There are always in the House of Commons a handful of MPs who, irrespective of party, have become so identified with their constituency that it is hard to imagine them apart. David is one (Bob Boothby in East Aberdeen, Aneurin Bevan in Ebbw Vale, Lady Astor in Plymouth Sutton were others). Such identification is seldom achieved without the MP establishing a kind of collective relationship with his constituents, of whatever party or none. This David has achieved with signal success, not from any sense of obligation but because, as a Border resident, he is, like the rest of us, interested in what goes on there. Happily for his constituents, this means they see a good deal of him; not only as a frequent speaker or guest of honour at some dinner or function but, more informally and often with Judy and the children, at agricultural show, canoe race, or Border common riding.

Liberal leaders of the past have been mostly men of unusual gifts, and the postwar trio of Grimond, Thorpe and Steel have been no exceptions. They have all shared a delightfully breezy approach to politics, a refusal to be portentous or solemn, to be other than the same people publicly as they are privately. They have been political enthusiasts rather than party propagandists, and this combined with vitality and eloquence has made them all outstanding communicators.

9

Within that framework they have greatly differed. Jo Grimond was always splendidly idiosyncratic; bubbling over with witticisms and ideas, charmingly withering about his opponents, companionable, vague, tweedy, dishevelled. It was Jo's succession to the leadership and his declared object of making the party a non-socialist, radical alternative to the Conservatives (which it always had been, but in the years following the great Labour landslide of 1945, needed courage to restate) that led me, and later David, to hoist our colours to his mast; and Jo's failure to make the breakthrough we were all hoping for in the '50s and '60s, resulted in the loss of a great political talent. Then there was Jeremy, exhibitionist extraordinary and mimic *par excellence*, ultimately another lost talent, but whose fall from grace should not obliterate his own great contribution to the party's fortunes – by so infecting Liberals up and down the country with his own enthusiasm and energies that in the election of February 1974 they delivered to him a record six million votes (and which resulted, under our present ludicrous electoral system, in a paltry fourteen parliamentary seats!).

And now there is David, as different from Jeremy as Jeremy was from Jo. Like them, he wears his office lightly; despite a heavy workload he never gives the impression of being other than good-humoured and self-assured, and with all the time in the world to give to whatever is in hand. Some politicians endeavour to scatter their enemies by bluster or scorn, but as Peter Bartram emphasises in this admirable assessment, David's way is one of quiet reasonableness.

This reasonableness stood David in good stead in interviews and broadcasts during the 1979 election campaign, and did much to reassure the more nervous in the party that the Lib-Lab pact had been a short-term *affaire* and not a permanent betrothal. (It was inspired by his belief that since one object of proportional representation is coalition and stable government, why object to making use of altered circumstances to practise what you preach?) David believes that no man of worth is immune to argument; and it is always a delight to watch him using his formidable skills as a debater to try and win a hostile or potentially hostile audience to his point of view. And it is a measure of his integrity and standing that whatever conclusions his audience may reach at the end, he is always listened to closely.

His other great political asset is his moral courage. He knew when he took on the abortion reform bill with a slim parliamentary majority that 3,000 Catholics in his constituency would disapprove of what he was doing. He knew, too, that his anti-apartheid stand against the Springbok rugby tour would endear him even less to the great rugby clubs of the Borders. On both issues he refused to compromise or retreat, believing that what he was doing was right. Fortunately, in the next election he kept his seat, though with a greatly reduced majority.

In every activity in life, timing is all; and it is David's great good fortune that he is leading the Liberal party at a moment of profound change in the make-up of British politics, a change as fundamental as that of the socialist upsurge at the expense of the Liberals during the inter-war years. Voters who feel frustrated by the continued see-saw dominance of the two main parties, and who long for co-operation in place of division, are coming to realise that the only way to achieve it is by supporting parties that believe in proportional representation. Hence the emergence of the SDP and the conclusions of the opinion polls that if they and the Liberals joined forces, there would be a real possibility of their forming the next government.

For David and others who have been toiling so long in the political wilderness, this is heady stuff. What for years seemed a remote pipe-dream could now, and soon, become reality. The next year or two will be a severe testing-time for both Liberals and Social Democrats, and I do not doubt that for his part David will conduct negotiations with his customary diplomacy and skill.

All the same, I trust he will not mind if I say this: although the Labour party manifesto of 1979, to which the SDP say they still adhere, was by no means the same as the Liberal party manifesto, the general public today would be hard put to spell out the differences between them. And they would be right. For on the main issues of the day – PR, the EEC, NATO, devolution, economic policy – *and most important of all, in their general political attitude of mind*, they are in broad agreement.

The country, therefore, will never forgive them if they fail to present a united front. It is, in my view, not good enough for candidates of the one party to stand for election with merely the support of the other. *Every* candidate, whether Liberal or SDP, who offers himself for election should do so under the banner of

11

'Liberal and SDP' or 'SDP and Liberal'. Failure to do so will encourage the voters to start worrying about the few things that divide them, instead of acknowledging, as joint party candidature would ensure, the many things that unite them. Joint candidature would prove to the electorate the depth of each party's seriousness and commitment. And who knows, perhaps one day the two parties will merge. What little divides Roy Jenkins from David Steel is no more than what divides Peter Walker from Margaret Thatcher, and far less than what divides Denis Healey from Tony Benn.

This book is a kind of half-term report on the Liberal leader; it charts his progress to date. Where his star will take him from now on, no one can say, for in politics nothing is certain. But I have a hunch that it will continue to rise, and that in x years from now David will look back from a dizzy height and recognise that this period of his life was only a preparation for what was to come.

Ludovic Kennedy
June 1981

Mr Kennedy is a former president of the National League of Young Liberals and a former member of the Liberal party Council. He fought Rochdale for the Liberals at the by-election of 1958 and the general election of 1959.

1

The rugged realist

The leadership of the Liberal party is arguably the worst job in British politics. The Liberal leader holds a position without power and precious little patronage. He gets no pay, apart from his ordinary parliamentary salary, unlike the Prime Minister and the leader of the Opposition. His meagre expenses depend entirely on what a perennially impoverished party organisation can scrape together at the time. At Westminster he occupies a poky office, like a converted corridor. He never works less than seventy hours a week, and frequently more than a hundred. Yet this grindingly hard effort is rarely appreciated by public, press or party members.

For much of the year, he is a stranger to his family, seeing them only for a few hours each weekend – and then only when constituency engagements do not intervene. And perhaps worst of all, after several years he is liable to be cast aside, as a bored public seeks a new face and new ideas. In an age of daily exposure through television and the press, few party leaders last more than a decade.

Despite this unattractive prospect, there is no shortage of applicants for the post of Liberal leader. Two candidates battled energetically for the post the last time it became vacant in 1976. When Jo Grimond surrendered his crown in 1967, there were three contenders. On each occasion the real ferocity of the battle for the leadership has made some observers think the contestants were fighting for a position of real national power and influence, rather than the top job in a party which has been frequently referred to by its enemies as little more than a pleasant debating society.

Yet despite the sneers, the fact remains that for most of this century the Liberal leadership has been held by a series of men of outstanding ability. Some, like Asquith and Lloyd George, have been major figures in British political history. But, oddly, all of them have been a curious mixture of heroic and tragic qualities, like characters out of a Shakespearean play. Most of them have seen their high hopes and ideals dashed, and ended their lives as disappointed men.

Throughout the century there has been a gulf between the ability and ultimate achievement of Liberal leaders. Campbell-Bannerman, so full of promise as leader of a radical government, died just two years into his premiership. The peace-loving Asquith drifted into the First World War, fell out with Lloyd George and eventually lost his parliamentary seat. Lloyd George himself, one of the most charismatic leaders of the century, finished up in the political wilderness, a prophet without followers. Sir Herbert Samuel presided over the final dismemberment of the Liberal party's once-great organisation. Sir Archibald Sinclair served his nation well in wartime as Minister for Air, only to be tossed aside by his ungrateful Caithness and Sutherland constituents when peace came. Clement Davies saw the Liberal party lose a record tally of deposits at the 1950 general election and Liberal support sink to its lowest level ever. Jo Grimond's dream of a realignment of radical forces in British politics faded when Labour won the 1966 general election with a handsome majority. Jeremy Thorpe quit politics broken-hearted after a sensational court case and alleged homosexual scandal.

Which brings us to the present incumbent, the Right Honourable David Steel, Privy Councillor, Member of Parliament, father of three, heir to the tradition of Gladstone and the ninth Liberal leader of the twentieth century. In more ways than one, Steel breaks the mould of previous Liberal leaders. He does not possess the commanding Olympian presence of an Asquith or a Grimond, or the super-sized ego of a Lloyd George or a Thorpe. *Daily Mail* columnist Anne Batt described him as 'just a nice, hard-working, reliable, Christian sort of chap.' Not the sort of chap, in short, that you would expect to find leading a political party, let alone the Liberal party. Unlike Jo Grimond, who married Asquith's granddaughter, Steel has no dynastic links with the great Liberal families; nor does he have the natural political background of Jeremy Thorpe, whose father was a Tory MP. But more than any of his predecessors as Liberal leader in the last half a century, he appreciates the changing role of the Liberal party, and understands how the job of the Liberal leader must also reflect that change. To pursue this important point more deeply, we need to survey the recent history of the Liberal party.

A political party in decline is a sad sight, and it is not uncommon for the members of a declining party to be slow in recognising that history has passed them by. When the Liberal party lost its status as one of the great parties of state in the 1920s, for several decades the leading members still acted as though the Liberals were a kind of government in exile, waiting in the wings for the nation's call at the next general election. In 1945 the Labour party came to power with its first majority government, finally dispelling any lingering doubts that it had supplanted the Liberals as the main party on the radical wing of British politics.

This was underlined at the 1950 general election, when Labour retained power with a hair's-breadth majority, and a record number of nearly four hundred Liberal candidates lost their deposits − fortunately all insured by Lloyd's of London. When Winston Churchill regained power in 1951, he offered Clement Davies, whose Liberals had polled a meagre 2.7 per cent of the popular vote in the general election, a seat in the cabinet. Davies preferred to maintain the Liberals' independence, and during the remainder of the fifties the Liberal party staggered on from crisis to crisis, a political home for the ageing remnants of the pre-war Liberal party, a few young hopefuls and some colourful cranks. When Jo Grimond became leader of the party in 1956, he recognised the need for new ideas and policies, and decided the Liberals should try to carve a role for themselves as a non-socialist, radical party. Grimond's espousal of these attractive ideas brought a number of new people of high ability into the party, including Steel himself, who joined while a student at Edinburgh University, and came to know Grimond well.

But Grimond ultimately failed to convince his Liberals that the test of realignment was whether the party could constructively co-operate with other radical forces in British politics. In 1965, when it seemed that the survival of Harold Wilson's Labour government would depend on Liberal votes, even the most tentative Grimond-like hint that he might be prepared to do a deal with Labour brought a storm of protest, mostly from middle-class Liberal activists in south and west of England constituencies. At the 1966 general election, Wilson comfortably increased his majority, and although the number of Liberal MPs went up, the Liberal vote in the country declined, and Grimond's dream of radical realignment became once more a distant prospect.

By 1974 the Liberal party, now led by an effervescent Jeremy Thorpe at the height of his powers, had polled more than six million votes, although it won only fourteen seats in the general election precipitated by Ted Heath's confrontation with the miners. After the election Heath summoned Thorpe to Downing Street to offer him a seat in the cabinet and other government posts, if the Liberals would vote to keep the Tory government alive. Although tempted, Thorpe rejected Heath's offer under pressure from party activists, and the Conservative government fell. In the interval between the February and October 1974 general elections, the Liberal party failed to come to grips with the political opportunity which lay within its grasp. At its September conference it agreed to campaign for an overall majority and accept the offer of coalition only on the most hedged-about terms. When the election came, the Liberal tide once again receded.

So by the end of 1974, the Liberal party had been in a position three times in less than twenty-five years to influence or participate in the government of Britain. This is a telling argument against those who say the Liberals are a spent force in British politics.

In both 1965 – when Grimond floated his idea – and in 1974, Steel, as a newly elected MP and later as chief whip, had been on the edge of the argument. He loyally supported his leaders on both occasions, but he had already developed a clearly defined idea about the role the Liberal party should play in British politics in the next few years.

Steel holds two views which are basically so simple and so self-evident that it is amazing they are not the received wisdom amongst all Liberal party members. The first is that as a small party, faced with the injustices of the first-past-the-post electoral system, the Liberal party will have to co-operate with one of the larger parties if it wants a taste of power. The second is that it is impossible for a party to believe in proportional representation – as the Liberals do – *and* support the primacy of single-party governments commanding overall parliamentary majorities. No government has been elected with more than 50 per cent of the popular vote since the 1930s, and no major European democracy manages to operate proportional representation without some form of multi-party government.

Steel's great contribution to Liberal politics so far has been to get these ideas accepted amongst party members, although there are still pockets of resistance. He achieved what both his immediate predecessors failed to do, which was to lead his party into some association with government – Jim Callaghan's faltering administration in 1977. Moreover, he extracted the party from the arrangement with its identity more or less intact, and fought a reasonably successful general election in 1979, at which the party emerged with a respectable popular vote and its parliamentary party basically still in one piece.

The traditional argument against Liberals used to be that no one knew what they stood for. Steel has started to change that – paradoxically, not by adopting more policies, but by concentrating on fewer issues. Liberals love to adopt lengthy resolutions, but Steel has tried to bring the party's policy-makers down to earth. He has encouraged them to focus their attention on a limited number of vital issues where Liberals can have some influence, rather than develop a rag-bag of impractical proposals.

In short, Steel has given the Liberal party a stiff dose of rugged realism. He has reminded his party that politics is the art of the possible, not the pursuit of the impossible dream. Once he has decided what he wants, he pursues his policy with unbending determination. Although most members of the parliamentary Liberal party were sceptical about entering the Lib-Lab pact in 1977, Steel cajoled them into it. Keeping the pact on the rails for eighteen months became virtually a single-handed balancing act for him.

Although a realist, with a genuine desire for power, Steel has never been afraid to espouse unpopular causes. In 1967, as one of the youngest Members in the House, he chose to push the highly controversial Abortion Act through Parliament, even though he had 3,000 Catholics in his own constituency. At the time, his majority was little more than 2,000. Three years later he opposed the South African's Springbok rugby tour of Britain, leading the campaign against it in his Roxburgh, Selkirk and Peebles constituency, where rugby is treated almost as a religion. That campaign brought him some of the rare hatred he has ever experienced, in his own constituency, but he managed to retain his seat at the following general election.

So what makes this man tick? In reality, Steel is a political hard case, one of the toughest in Britain today. The gentle demeanour, the softly spoken voice, the air of sweet reason mask an inner core of sheer political determination – Steel by name, and steel by nature.

Under fire, he is one of Britain's most effective politicians. During his piloting of the Abortion Act through Parliament, he was subject to some of the vilest abuse ever thrown at a British politician. He was branded a child-murderer and a Herod by some opponents of the legislation. A decade later, the taunt turned to 'Judas', when he led the Liberals into the Lib-Lab pact. Day after day, Steel was subjected to a torrent of criticism and abuse published in Britain's Tory tabloids. Amazingly, Steel does not wilt or waver under this kind of pressure. Even more important in a party leader, when the going gets rough he keeps calm and his judgement remains sound.

Yet although Steel can provoke the strongest of reactions from both supporters and opponents, most of the time he comes across to Mr and Mrs Average Voter as the archetypal reasonable man – he is the politician most likely to evoke a favourable response from a British public which likes its politicians moderate, not militant. Steel frequently tops the popularity polls as the party leader of whom voters most approve. This may be partly because he rarely gets called on, as do ministers in government, to take unpopular decisions. Yet even during the days of the Lib-Lab pact, when some of the press were eager to heap all the blame for Britain's ills on the Liberals, Steel's popularity still ran way ahead of his party's.

How can a man emerge from the crucible of political controversy time after time, and not burn himself up? Steel works incredibly hard – longer hours than most other MPs – but this is part of his nature. As the son of a minister of the Church of Scotland, he was brought up to believe in the Presbyterian values of thrift, hard work and purity. Former party leader Jeremy Thorpe, who worked closely with Steel in Parliament for eleven years, believes a study of Steel's upbringing unlocks many of the clues to his character. Sons of the Manse are, after all, by reputation, sturdy, independent boys who know right from wrong.

When he was eleven, Steel began to see something of the world, as his father took the family to live in East Africa, where he was a minister of the Church. Only a few years later, Steel returned to boarding school in Edinburgh, so from a young age he developed a taste for independence and self-reliance.

The most perceptive insight into Steel's character comes from his devoted wife, Judy. He is able to keep cool in a crisis because he knows when he is right and trusts his judgement over other people's, she says. His determination and drive stem from a deep inner belief in the rightness of his judgements. What to some people might seem stubbornness is, for Steel, the simple working out of ideas which are self-evident.

One of the remarkable features of Steel's political career has been the consistency of his political opinions. Columnist Frank Johnson once criticised Steel for having 'espoused every safe, fatuously modish cause of his time with an alacrity which has made lemmings appear cautious.' In fact, this is far less true of Steel than of most other politicians from all parties.

The main theme of Steel's political life has been the radical realignment of British politics. It was Jo Grimond's espousal of this principle which originally brought him into the Liberal party. And he has pursued the idea of realignment, through the abortive Radical Action Movement of the late 1960s, the Lib-Lab pact of the late 1970s, to the current co-operation between the Liberal and Social Democratic parties. In an article he wrote for the party's newspaper, *Liberal News*, and entitled 'Why I came into politics', Steel said, 'I came to Parliament to stop the see-saw politics at Westminster. I saw how damaging to Britain were the alternating lurches to the left and right.'

On policy issues, Steel is most interested in foreign affairs. He takes a particularly close interest in issues connected with the Third World, where he has travelled extensively, and where he has many friends. He is a noted advocate of human rights, and a consistent and active campaigner against South Africa's apartheid regime. He was banned from visiting Rhodesia by the illegal Smith regime, a mark of considerable distinction amongst anti-apartheid campaigners.

On home issues, Steel is at his most persuasive when he is arguing the Liberal case for electoral reform, which he does in an almost non-political, bi-partisan way. Steel is at his weakest when talking about economics. Although not quite in the Alec Douglas-Home matchstick class of economists, for most of his career he has had only a general grasp of the main issues of British economic policy. Until the 1979 general election, Steel relied heavily for his economic background on the ebullient John Pardoe, the party's deputy leader and Treasury spokesman. Pardoe's defeat in 1979 was a cruel blow to Steel.

Steel is very much a politician of the television age. Apart from Jeremy Thorpe, he is the only British party leader to have worked professionally, on screen, for a television company, before entering politics. As a result he is an effective television performer, especially in interviews or panel discussions. His party political broadcasts, although generally reckoned effective, tend to suffer from an excess of elder-statesman-style *gravitas*.

The age of the platform orator has largely passed, and Steel reflects this. He is a convincing public speaker, and relies on arguing a closely reasoned case which appeals to his audience's intellect, rather than turning on the passion to appeal to their hearts. He can be amusing, but is not a natural wit in the style of Jeremy Thorpe or Norman St John Stevas. Some of his best jokes are written for him by his small coterie of unpaid speech-writers. Like Ted Heath, he is inclined to laugh uproariously at his own jokes.

Meeting Steel is like being introduced to a cleverer than average small-town solicitor – which he could well have become had he not entered politics. He greets you politely and almost diffidently, with no hint of pretension or self-importance. Everyone who knows him agrees that he has absolutely no 'side'.

At five feet nine inches, Steel stands rather less than average height. He weighs nearly eleven stone, two stone more than the slimline Steel who first entered Parliament in 1965. Steel is no snappy dresser, although he looks neat, and has won the Scottish tailors' award as Scotland's best-dressed man. The natural Steel predilection is for a suit of conservative cut and cloth, and a sober tie. The one sartorial departure from this is a taste for heavily striped shirts which went out of fashion more than a decade ago.

In the House of Commons, Steel is well liked by a large number of Members in all parties. He is what is known as a House of Commons man, a politician who does not pursue political differences and grudges outside the chamber to the detriment of personal relationships with other Members. Steel recognises pragmatically that if, as a member of a minority party, he is to get things done, he needs to establish common ground with members of other parties.

His relationships have not always been so good with some of his own party. Steel has never had much time for committee room wafflers, of which there are a large number in the Liberal party. He gets especially irritated by the impractical ideas and suggestions which come from some of the party committees, and he was particularly annoyed by some of the criticisms of his conduct of the Lib-Lab pact which emerged from Liberal party committees. The committee members simply did not understand the practical problems of the situation, he said. Holding views such as these, Steel has not always been a punctilious attender of party committee meetings, a fact which has also earned him criticism from time to time.

However, the secret of Steel's success is that he directs energies where they can be most effective, and this is more likely to be in the House of Commons, his own constituency or in cross-party meetings, than in his own party committees.

Many pundits predicted that the Liberal party would slide into decline under Steel's leadership. When he took the party into the Lib-Lab pact, they said it was finished as an electoral force, and stood little chance of holding any seats at the succeeding general election. Instead, the Liberal party today, largely as a result of Steel's leadership strategy, stands on the brink of some of the most exciting political developments it has experienced for half a century or more. Far from being extinct, the Liberal party is now in a more cohesive and healthy state than at any time for a generation. Steel is the first Liberal leader for fifty years to have identified a clear role for the party and to have set about carving out that role in British politics with hard-headed and pragmatic determination. For a 43-year-old leader who inherited a dispirited party, this is a significant achievement. Indeed, Steel is well on his way to being the most important leader of the Liberal party since Lloyd George.

2

The makings of a radical

David Martin Scott Steel, the modest son of the Manse who became the youngest ever leader of the Liberal party, was born on 31 March 1938. He was to be the eldest of five children born to David and Sheila Steel. His parents, both true Scots, had met whilst undergraduates at Aberdeen University, and married in 1937. David Steel senior, now a triple graduate from Aberdeen, entered the ministry, and was later to rise high in the Church of Scotland. He became a Moderator of the Church of Scotland in 1974.

But in 1938, Mr Steel, while still a young minister, had been sent to tend a flock in Buckhaven, Fife, a small mining town on the north bank of the Firth of Forth. It was from the Manse in Buckhaven that Sheila Steel departed a few days before the birth of her first child was due, to the Forth Maternity Hospital, Kirkcaldy. It was here at around noon on the 31 March that the lusty infant Steel weighed in at six pounds eight ounces. Baby David and his mother spent about two weeks in the Forth Maternity Hospital – for a first birth, par for the course in those pre-war days – before returning to the Manse at Buckhaven and to a controversy.

David Steel has been at the centre of many fierce political controversies throughout his political life. And he started life the centre of an argument over what he should be named. His mother had set her heart on Ian – Ian being the Gaelic for John, the baby's maternal grandfather's name. But his father had his own ideas about the rules of precedence which should apply in the naming of his first born. In *his* family, the first son had always been named after his paternal grandfather – in this case, David. Martin was chosen as his mother's maiden name, and Scott as his paternal grandmother's maiden name. So it was David Martin Scott Steel that his father christened in the Kirk at Buckhaven a few weeks later.

David Steel comes from a long line of David Steels which stretches back at least to the late seventeenth century. The first noted David Steel which history records was a Scottish Covenanter who was shot on 20 December 1686. A monument to the Covenanter David Steel still stands at Upper Skelly Hill, Lanarkshire. So far, the latest David Steel has not had the time to pay his respects, although he is always meaning to fit in a visit to the remains of this notorious forebear.

However, most of the intervening David Steels have made little or no mark on the face of history. Although the Steels of Buckhaven would probably have been regarded as middle class by the rest of the inhabitants of the burgh, that would have been because of Mr Steel's position in the community rather than the size of his bank balance. In fact, the Steel antecedents are distinctly working class, in sharp contrast with previous Liberal party leaders'.

Mr Steel's father started work as a shop boy in the Co-op. By dint of hard work and application, he worked his way up to manager. Margaret Thatcher has the distinction of being a grocer's daughter; David Steel is a grocer's grandson − although Mrs Thatcher's father owned the shop, while Mr Steel remained a successful employee. David's maternal grandfather was a primary school headmaster.

Throughout most of their young life in the 1930s and '40s, the Steels struggled to make ends meet. They would live in huge, draughty, Scottish Manses, built in an age of domestic servants. Yet somehow Mrs Steel managed to run these houses with only occasional assistance from a mother's help. Few, if any, can have been very notable, for David remembers none of them.

In 1941, when David was three, the Steels moved to Dumbarton on Clydeside. By now the war had come to Scotland, and the Clydeside shipyards were a favoured target for Goering's bombers. On many nights the Steels watched, horrified, as the shipyards in Greenock, just across the Clyde from Dumbarton, were pounded by Nazi bombs.

Mercifully, Dumbarton was only subjected to a major bombing raid once during the Steels' residence. On that occasion, a bomb landed across the road from the Manse and demolished two houses. The Manse itself suffered from broken windows and other slight damage, and incendiaries dropped into the garden.

During these raids, Mr Steel would be out helping the emergency services, and providing comfort to those injured, or to relatives of the bereaved. The rest of the family would retreat to a kind of converted wine cellar under the old Victorian Manse. This contained beds for Mrs Steel, David and his baby brother, Michael. The family reached this haven by scrambling through a wooden trap door. In the event of a bomb directly hitting the house, it is probable they would have been incarcerated in this cellar, as in a tomb. David's earliest memory of childhood is of sitting on an orange box in the cellar dimly lit by candles, listening to the thunder of bombs above, and waiting for the all-clear to sound.

Psychiatrists claim that the basic essentials of a person's character are determined by the age of five or six. After that, although there may be a change of balance, the fundamentals are fixed. Like many psychiatric theories, this may or may not be valid. But if it is, it is interesting to note Mrs Steel's verdict on her five-year-old son. He was a quiet, thoughtful, well-behaved little boy who nevertheless had a mind of his own. 'He was a very passive good child,' remembers Mrs Steel. 'David was always a very easy child to manage'. When he got into mischief, it was normally as a result of a prank devised by his more adventurous younger brother Michael. Although David had two brothers and two sisters, he was closest to Michael, now a highly respected doctor researching into cancer.

At school David was a slow starter – often the case with first children – but one day everything clicked into place, and thereafter he held his own. At the age of five he had been despatched to the local school, Dumbarton Academy, where he was taught the rudiments of reading, writing and arithmetic in a good old-fashioned way by a Miss Henderson. David enjoyed reading, and books became a major interest in his childhood. So did cars. He adored a pedal car given to him by his parents. And he was driving a real car around fields by the age of thirteen. He still has a penchant for fast driving, which on more than one occasion has brought a brush with the law.

Although a quiet, somewhat reserved child, David could, on occasion, display remarkable initiative for one so young. When he was six, his mother took him on a visit to Glasgow to be measured for his first kilt – a big event for a young Scottish boy. On the journey David saw a flower-seller – a new experience for a child who had previously only known of flowers that grew in the garden. He was amazed when his mother told him that people paid money for the seller's flowers. Later that day, after they had returned to the Manse, Mrs Steel missed David. He was found near the local railway station, selling bunches of wilted bluebells, plucked from the Steels' garden, to commuters returning from work. He had already taken one shilling and ten pence – a shilling of it from the local provost who admired the young lad's free-enterprise spirit.

Towards the end of the war the Steels moved to Edinburgh, where Mr Steel took an appointment in the Church of Scotland headquarters at 121 George Street. David transferred to James Gillespie's Boys School, a traditional establishment founded by an Edinburgh merchant but by then an ordinary local authority primary school. At this school David made steady academic progress, without ever showing sparkling aptitude for any one subject. Mrs Steel recalls that he used to get comments like 'could do better' written on his school reports. He did well enough, however, to win a scholarship to George Watson's College, one of Edinburgh's brightest academic institutions. But before David could take his place there, Mr Steel was offered, and accepted, the post of minister for the East African territories – Kenya, Uganda and Tanganyika, as it was then known, now Tanzania. For David, this marked the biggest change in his life so far. And it came at a time in his life – he had just turned eleven – when he was about to discover ideas and to develop opinions of his own. Although he only spent four years in Nairobi, from the age of eleven to fifteen, this period has had a very fundamental influence on Steel's approach to political life – and to people.

We need to pause in the narrative at this point, and consider the kind of boy who was to make the three-week voyage by British Indian lines via Suez, with the rest of his family. By now David had emerged as a true son of the Manse – a young boy reserved in character, yet with a mind of his own, a streak of independence and a strong sense of equality. What it means to be a son of the Manse, can best be described by Mr Steel. 'A Manse child has considerable advantages over others in that he meets all kinds of people from all strata of society in the Manse. He might be meeting the Lord Lieutenant one minute and a miner the next, and he's taught to treat all people automatically the same way.

Manse society is a very democratic society'.

Furthermore, David had been growing up in a radical household. Although Mr and Mrs Steel regarded themselves as floating voters, it is unlikely they ever floated far enough right to vote Conservative. Most of their votes during the 1930s, '40s and '50s would have been cast for Labour candidates. The only periodical David can remember seeing around his home was the staunchly socialist *New Statesman*. Nor was Mr Steel ever squeamish about bringing politics into his sermons. The Church of Scotland has, of course, always been more radical than the Church of England, often described as the Tory party at prayer. As Mr Steel puts it, 'The Church of Scotland has never been tied to any one party, but has worked on the general principle that every government is wrong. So we don't have much of this talk in Scotland that the Church should keep out of politics, which is nonsense because it means that politics has nothing to do with morality.'

In his sermons Mr Steel had never been shy about applying a Christian critique to local and national situations. When an election came, Mr Steel did not hesitate to advise his parishioners on the general principles they should bear in mind before they cast their ballots. If anyone accused him of advising his flock to vote Labour, he would claim that was only their interpretation of what he had said. 'If you think the Tories are so dreadful they can't stand a Christian critique, then you've made your judgement,' he would tell them.

It was in this radical atmosphere that David had been growing up, noting, with appropriate filial devotion, what his father had to say at home and in his sermons about the issues of the day. So even by the time David left with his family for Nairobi, he was used to looking at events with a radical eye.

The effect of the four years spent in Kenya was to reinforce David's basic radicalism – and also to give him a lifelong detestation of racial prejudice. The Steels arrived in their new Manse – close to the centre of Nairobi – at a time when the sun was setting on the British Empire in many parts of the world. Yet old attitudes lingered on amongst the colonial settlers. David was enrolled at the Prince of Wales School in Nairobi. The school was racially segregated – whites only. Steel says today, 'One of the remarkable features of colonial education was that it was completely segregated. Although we condemn it in South Africa, it happened in British colonies.'

This made a deep impression on the young David. He says, 'The only social contact that I had with Africans and Asians was through things like YMCA camps and the Boys Brigade. But that was exceptional. Most of the European children had no social contact with African or Asian children – they may have met the farmworkers' children, but not socially – and that was one of the things that made me political.'

Steel says he first started to develop an interest in current affairs during his time in Kenya. This is hardly surprising, for Kenya was passing through a turbulent period – the last few years of colonial administration before independence. The Mau Mau terrorised much of the country, and although Nairobi was comparatively safer, the Steels took strict security precautions. Doors were kept firmly locked, and children were never left alone in the house. Mr Steel slept with a revolver by his bed. Mrs Steel favoured a shotgun. She reckoned she was such a bad shot, she could not hit a moving target with a revolver. Fortunately, she never had to try.

Although travelling to some parts of the country was definitely dangerous, this did not stop Mr Steel conducting services in all parts of the country. On one occasion, a group of Africans arrived for an impromptu service out in the bush with Sten guns, which they kept under the pews during the sermons and hymns. Mr Steel preached Christ's message of love and peace with a revolver hidden under his cassock.

Yet despite these dangers, Mr Steel had considerable sympathy for the Africans, and was a constant critic of the British colonial administration. He was especially critical of the administration's policy of keeping detainees in camps without trial. Mr Steel railed against these policies in his sermons, and in a weekly broadcast sermon heard on Kenyan radio by thousands of listeners. This ruffled the administration, which considered expelling the Steel family, but this plan was forestalled when a senior member of the administration threatened to resign. Years later, when Mr Steel returned on a visit to Kenya as Moderator of the Church of Scotland, he received a presidential summons from Jomo Kenyatta, one of the African leaders who had been detained by the British colonial administration. At the end of an informal talk, Mr Steel asked why he had been sent for. Kenyatta replied, 'Because when I was in prison I had a transistor radio and used to listen to your sermons, and you gave me courage and hope.'

During his period in Kenya, David passed from childhood to adolescence. He developed an intense earnestness, of a kind which often comes over young people as they grow up. He performed well at school, without being especially brilliant in any subject. He was better at arts subjects than science or practical activities like woodwork. He enjoyed reading and acting. One play he appeared in at school was called *The Man in the Bowler Hat*. He played the chief villain, a role the Tories were later to mark out for him in his political life.

He also wrote intense, obscure poetry. A sample from one of his poems, entitled 'With Purpose But No Head', runs:
'Suspect, revile, press on and play the game;
We know we are
Harp players always playing
Safe at home.
We run, we flee and make towards the lair.'
Fortunately, Steel has never pursued a career as a poet.

By the time David was fifteen, his parents realised that his education had reached a critical point. The Steels hoped David would go on to university – a Scottish university, naturally. There was no big decision about this; the Steels had always been a family who attended university, and David's parents assumed he would want to do likewise. If David was to enter a Scottish university, the Steels considered it was probably best that he prepared for this in Scotland. So David got ready to return to Scotland to take his place at George Watson's as a boarding pupil. It meant leaving his family for the first time in his life. It also meant saying goodbye to an especially loved pet monkey. With characteristic resourcefulness, David had written to Edinburgh Zoo asking if they would like to have the animal. But the zoo had declined the offer of a free monkey.

When David entered George Watson's his independence and interest in politics really blossomed. In Kenya, David's life had revolved round a small circle of friends in a fairly closed and introspective community. Now David became aware of the broader sweep of human affairs for the first time. Kenya and the racial situation there had made him political in a vague sort of way. At George Watson's his political feelings started to crystalise. He joined the school debating society, and soon became a regular contributor to debates. He also had the chance to hear prominent visiting guest speakers, like Lord Kilmuir, the Conservative Lord Chancellor, and W. S. Morrison, Speaker of the House of Commons. The debating society took on other schools, and David played a key role in these contests. He also became vice-chairman of the Edinburgh Schools Citizenship Association — a branch of the Junior United Nations Association. His parents had been aware only from his letters of his growing interest in politics and debating. When they returned to Edinburgh, they heard him speak. His mother recalls, 'It was really quite a brilliant speech. We regretted we hadn't got a tape recorder to record it.'

David did not see his father for four years, and he saw his mother only once while he was at George Watson's. His parents could not afford fares to Kenya for school holidays. During this period, David visited his father's parents every week at their Edinburgh tenement flat. He also regularly visited his father's sister, Lizbeth, an Edinburgh primary school teacher. Many of the school holidays were spent with his mother's parents in Aberdeen.

At this time, although David tended to take a fairly radical view of political issues, he was not allied to any one political party. It is not easy to pinpoint exactly when he first regarded himself as a Liberal. He cannot really remember himself. But perhaps it came at a fairly insignificant parliamentary by-election which took place in the Edinburgh South constituency on 29 May 1957. The by-election was caused by the resignation of Sir William Darling, who had represented the constituency since 1945, and who, like Steel, was a former pupil of James Gillespie's School. His only significant achievement in the Commons had been to sponsor the Public Libraries (Scotland) Act. And his 12,000 majority over Labour was reckoned, correctly, to be unassailable. The one point of interest in an otherwise dull by-election was the intervention of Liberal candidate William Douglas Home.

Douglas Home, the third son of the 13th Earl of Home, was also the brother of the 14th Earl, later Sir Alec Douglas Home and briefly Conservative Prime Minister in the early 1960s. On the face of it, his aristocratic background and Eton and Oxford education seemed unlikely to appeal to the youthful, radical David. Yet Douglas Home was a colourful, almost charismatic figure, with a streak of radicalism of his own. He had already become a noted playwright. During the war he had unsuccessfully fought three parliamentary by-elections as an independent, during the by-election truce called by the main political parties. And in Edinburgh South he was fighting a lively campaign.

This was enough for David, who had been appointed editor of the school newspaper. He penned a vigorous editorial, supporting Douglas Home's candidature. David's arguments in favour of Douglas Home centred not so much round a basic adherence to Liberalism as support for his brilliance as a parliamentary candidate. Despite the young Steel's editorial endorsement, Douglas Home flopped into third place on polling day, 7,000 votes behind the victorious Conservative candidate.

It is worth noting here a small irony in Steel's life – the influence the Douglas Home family has had at two important junctures of his career. As we have seen, it was William who first sparked David's interest in the Liberal party. And it was the unpopularity of the Tories during Alec's leadership which was a decisive factor in helping Steel to gain his Roxburgh, Selkirk and Peebles constituency at the second attempt, in 1965.

However, while debating took up a great deal of David's time, there was still a career to think of. Years earlier, when asked by a teacher what he wanted to do when he grew up, he had replied that he wanted to be on radio. Now his ambitions centred on more prosaic career possibilities. Before he left Kenya, he had had a long talk with his father about his future. He had told his father that he was considering a career as a minister of the Church, as a doctor or a teacher. His father pointed out that David would have to pass through the same educational doors to reach each career. So his education in the sixth form at George Watson's was clearly mapped out for him. In the event, David sat the exams for five highers – the Scottish equivalent of A levels – in English, mathematics, Latin, Greek and French. He passed all, which proved more than adequate to ensure his admittance to Edinburgh University. He enrolled at the university in the autumn of 1957.

David obtained two degrees while at university: an Ordinary Scottish MA degree, a sort of general-purpose degree which involved studying history, mathematics, philosophy, civil law, Latin and some other subjects; and a law degree – Bachelor of Laws. He spent the first three years of his university career gaining his first degree, and two more years obtaining his law degree. Yet the importance of university in David's life does not lie solely in its academic opportunities. He has never been a brilliant academic performer, although his achievements have been perfectly respectable, especially when set against the fact that he devoted much of his later school and university time to 'outside' activities such as debating clubs and political societies.

For David, George Watson's had provided a sound education, but more importantly, it had given him a grounding in working with other people, had stimulated his interest in public affairs, and started to equip him with some of the techniques he would need later in public life, such as public speaking. At university Steel built upon this solid foundation. He swiftly emerged as a leading university politician, both popular and effective. He fought and won some important battles on behalf of the students. And he firmly allied himself to the Liberal party.

Steel joined the Liberals as soon as he went up to Edinburgh. He signed up with the university Liberal Club, at that time enjoying a revival after years in the doldrums. Not too much should be read into his membership, however. In the late 1950s and 1960s, some students joined the political clubs of all three parties at university, just to find out what was happening, although Steel never joined the Conservatives or Labour. So why did he join the Liberals? He says, 'I knew I wasn't Tory and I knew I wasn't Labour, and rather negatively joined the Liberals. Through attending their meetings and hearing from those who were more committed than I was, and from visiting speakers, I became more positively committed.'

Steel also experienced his first election contest. It nearly ended in disaster. He had decided to stand as a first-year representative of the Student Representative Council. With just seven candidates for three seats, and with a long Edinburgh background behind him, he felt confident of victory. However, two new students, both from London, fought a brilliant campaign, and forced him into third place. He won a seat on the Council, but only just. He learnt an important lesson from that – never to treat any election campaign complacently.

Three years after entering university, Steel became President of the Student Representative Council. This is the equivalent of President of the union in an English university. He was the last 'part-time' President Edinburgh ever had. During his term he persuaded the university authorities to allow the President a sabbatical year. He pointed out that he had risked his degree to perform his duties as President, which were important to the overall functioning of the university. The authorities accepted this argument. Steel also played a part in putting student views on the planning of a new student hall of residence.

However, Steel's most significant achievement at Edinburgh concerned the election and installation of a new Rector. The Rector occupies a position in Scottish universities which is unknown in their English equivalents. The Rector is chairman of the university governing body and also represents the interests of the students by whom he is elected. Over the years a parade of the famous and the infamous have been elected as Rectors. Sometimes the rectorial contests devolve into party political fights. On other occasions, non-political candidates, such as actors or authors, dominate the campaigns.

Inevitably, the campaigns are fought with considerable zest by the students. Steel, who by now had become more closely involved with the Scottish Liberal party, persuaded Jo Grimond, at this time at the height of his powers as leader of the Liberal party, to stand as a candidate. His opponents were Roy Thomson, the Canadian newspaper proprietor, and Philip Noel-Baker, the respected Labour MP. Steel set about organising the Grimond campaign with efficient determination. But there were wider issues, in Steel's view, than the election of Grimond.

In previous years, the office of Rector had been brought into disrepute – or so it was said – by the behaviour of some students at rectorial elections and at the subsequent installation cer-emonies. A traditional feature of Edinburgh rectorial cam-paigns was a student fight in the university quad, at which supporters of the rival candidates hurled bags of flour and rotten eggs at one another, and tried to slip soot-covered cod's heads down each other's trousers. At rectorial installations, behaviour had been equally boisterous. At the previous rectorial installation for the bearded actor James Robertson Justice, in 1958, a barrage of flour bombs and tomatoes had been hurled at the platform, and a toilet roll had landed at the feet of Prince Philip, Chancellor of the University. At Glasgow University, Tory Home Secretary R. A. Butler had been struck full in the face with a flour bomb whilst trying to make his rectorial address, and had been unable to finish his speech.

By today's standards – after students have been shot on American campuses, and sit-ins have become so common they do not even hit the headlines, and flour bombs have been replaced by petrol bombs – these activities seem amusing, and even trivial. But in the buttoned-up climate of the early 1960s, it was just not on. Small wonder, then, that there was serious talk of doing away with the office of Rector.

Steel viewed this with alarm, but recognised that if the office was to be saved, the students would have to rescue it by their own example. So during the campaign and after, Steel emerged as a political hard man, berating the students with their previous bad behaviour, and urging a more sedate approach to the campaign. A pro-Grimond pamphlet, almost certainly penned by Steel, read, 'The big issue in this rectorial may prove to be not the election of a Rector for the next three years but the office of Rector itself. The right to elect a Rector is a traditional and intensely democratic one which must be jealously guarded if we are to retain it in full measure. We, the student body, must ensure in the coming campaign that nothing in our behaviour calls into disrepute the high office of Lord Rector nor antagonises university or civic authorities towards it.'

Grimond sailed home with 1,907 votes, a 1,060 majority over his nearest rival, Roy Thomson, with Philip Noel-Baker bringing up the rear with just 544 votes. A statement issued by the Student Representative Council after the result was announced, which bears the stamp of Steel about it, noted 'with satisfaction' that there had been no painting on university buildings during the campaign and no damage to persons or property. 'For the first time in many years no students have been arrested by the police, or subject to disciplinary action by the university authorities. All this makes us feel that the rectorship has been given a new lease of respectable life in the eyes of the public,' the statement added.

However, the comparatively peaceful election of a new Rector failed to impress the university authorities. They threatened to end the traditional installation ceremony, and ban students from using the McEwen Hall, the usual venue, for the ceremony. As Senior President of the Student Representative Council, Steel sought a mandate from the students to negotiate with the university authorities. At a mass meeting of students, he told them, 'There is nothing particularly amusing and nothing particularly funny in inviting a distinguished man to be Rector and then giving him dog's abuse when he comes.' Steel's plan was to turn the rectorial installation into a formal occasion. Steel bluntly instructed his student colleagues who planned to attend the installation to turn up properly dressed. A written instruction to all students stated, 'Men should wear lounge suits with white shirts, collar and tie. Dark blazer is a very suitable alternative. Women should wear appropriate dress, such as a suit, or a blazer and skirt.'

Steel also asked the students to vote in advance on a proposal from him not to throw missiles such as rotten fruit at the Rector and to try to stop anyone else throwing similar missiles. In the event, Grimond just faced some vigorous but good-natured heckling and a few paper darts when he made his rectorial speech. Steel persuaded the university authorities to relent and allow the McEwen Hall to be used, by showing that the students had pledged themselves to better behaviour and by arguing that, in any event, the authorities had agreed to the installation previously and could not now back down without breaking their word. An admiring John Mackintosh, a lecturer at the university, later to become a Labour MP, applauded Steel's victory. 'The great thing about student politics is that it teaches you to deal with rogues and villains,' he counselled Steel.

Steel gained a great deal from university which was of value to him in his later political career. He developed a kind of pragmatic approach to working with people of other political views in order to get things done. This is an important theme which recurs time and again throughout Steel's political life. For Steel, now due to leave university, that political life was about to begin.

3

First steps in a career

There is a strong amateur tradition in British politics. This is highlighted by the fact that Parliament assembles at two thirty in the afternoon, leaving the mornings free for Members to attend to other duties – some, for example, are company directors, farmers, something in the City, or trade union officials. David Steel runs sharply counter to this tradition. He is about the nearest the British ever come to being a professional politician.

All his adult life has been devoted to politics. He has only ever had one full-time job that was not connected with politics – and that with the BBC for less than six months. Yet Steel did not set out to become a political professional. We have seen that he had considered the possibility of a career in the Church, the law or teaching. Between the time he first discussed these ideas with his father and taking his first degree, he had decided that he was not called to the ministry, and that teaching was likely to be too dull. This left the law. He considered becoming an advocate, but a young advocate needs a private income for the first few years, before the lucrative briefs start to roll in. Steel's family certainly could not provide a private income. Indeed, Steel had few enough bawbees in his sporran during his university years. He supplemented his student grant by taking on a succession of holiday jobs, including selling ice-creams in Princes Street, Edinburgh.

As his university life came to an end, in the late spring of 1962, Steel searched for a career. Already he had vaguely considered the possibility of politics and of standing for election as an MP.

While still in his third year at university, the East Fife Liberal Association had asked him to be their prospective parliamentary candidate. He was tempted to fight Asquith's former seat, especially as he had been born in the constituency and knew it well. But the seat was hardly promising territory for the Liberal party, and Steel already faced the combined pressures of university politics and taking his degree. He turned the East Fife Liberals down.

The following year, he got the chance to stand as prospective parliamentary Liberal candidate for Edinburgh Pentlands – also a constituency he knew well. As he did not plan to take an especially active part in university politics in his fifth and final year, he felt free to take this on.

So in October 1961, while still a graduate student at Edinburgh, he was adopted as the prospective parliamentary Liberal candidate for Edinburgh Pentlands. This marked an important shift of emphasis in Steel's political work. Up until now, he had been mainly concerned with political life of the university, fighting battles such as the rectorial campaign. From now on, he devoted most of his energies in political work to the Liberal party. Steel had, in fact, been quietly building up his contacts and position in the Liberal party ever since he joined it immediately after going up to university. He had joined a canvassing party in a by-election in East Aberdeenshire, in 1958, caused by the elevation of Robert Boothby to the Lords – it was the first time he had ever knocked on doors for the Liberals. A year later he organised teams of canvassers to help the Liberal candidate the Honourable Simon Mackay (now Lord Tanlaw) in the Galloway by-election. Within the university, he had been elected President of the thriving University Liberal Club. In this capacity he attended meetings of the Scottish Liberal Party, and was elected to the Party's Executive Committee in July 1960.

However, despite his increasingly close involvement with the party in Scotland and in his Pentlands constituency, he had not considered politics as a career. Indeed, in 1962, despite the heady optimism created in the party by the Orpington by-election, when Liberal Eric Lubbock (now Lord Avebury) replaced a 15,000 Conservative majority with a 7,000 Liberal majority, few Members could expect to make a living out of professional politics. The number of full-time officials in the Scottish Liberal Party in the early 1960s could be counted on the fingers of one hand. South of the border, Steel was still unknown, so he could count on little prospect of employment by the slightly better organised English Liberal party.

In the spring of 1962, in search of gainful employment, Steel visited his university careers' officer. The career prospects did not appear particularly bright, for Steel had hardly distinguished himself academically at the university. He gained only pass degrees, the last floor down before the ignominious basement of failure. He managed neither credits nor distinctions in his finals. This is hardly surprising in view of Steel's full-hearted involvement in university and political life. Nor is it necessarily a point of criticism. People go to university for a variety of reasons – some to achieve academic distinction, some to seek fame or friendship, some merely to while away a few pleasant years. Steel felt that although he had not achieved the academic success of others, he had at least gained two degrees, and made a significant mark on the life of the university.

But this did not solve his immediate career problem. The university careers' officer made few imaginative suggestions. There were, apparently, career openings as a management trainee at two of Britain's leading companies, Shell and Plessey. This was distinctly unappealing to Steel, and he did not bother to attend the interviews. Slightly more attractive was the idea of a post in university administration at St Andrews. But nothing came of this, for in the meantime two leading members of the Scottish Liberal party, George Mackie (now Lord Mackie), Chairman of the Executive Committee, and Arthur Purdom, the General Secretary, had heard that Steel was seeking a post in administration.

In the rosy post-Orpington days, and with a general election possibly only two years away, the Scottish Liberal party chiefs had decided it was time to strengthen their slender professional organisation. In May 1962 they appointed Steel as Assistant Secretary to the party at a salary of £850 per annum on a contract which ran until the next general election. Steel was given special responsibility for publicity, publications and local government affairs. The object of the appointment was to relieve Arthur Purdom of some of his administrative duties so he could spend more time travelling around the constituencies.

The post offered Steel a job which he could enjoy and in which he could shine. The appointment came as a great relief to him, not least because he had become engaged and planned to marry later in the year.

Steel had first met Judy MacGregor as a first-year student at the university. They had attended the same classes together, but were on no more than a nodding acquaintanceship. Judy says, 'I first really noticed him when he made a speech.' In their third year, both served on the Student Representative Council, but, according to Judy, they did not get on well.

Fittingly, it was the Liberal party and, more especially, Jo Grimond, who brought them together. Both had been invited to Grimond's rectorial dinner in 1961, and Judy found herself seated next to Steel. They found they had many interests in common, and in the ensuing months friendship blossomed into romance. Their friends thought they were made for each other. And it is easy to see why. David was captivated by Judy. Judy was a vivacious girl with auburn hair and an especially pretty smile. She shared many of David's radical views and, like David, felt motivated to work for them. She was studying for a law degree, and planned to become a solicitor. The couple became engaged in March 1962, shortly before they left university. Judy's family lived in Dunblane, Perthshire. Her father was a retired expert in forestry and had received the CBE for colonial service in West Africa. The couple were married at Dunblane Cathedral in October 1962 at a ceremony attended by two hundred guests. The service was conducted by David's father. The newly weds spent the whole of their savings, just £60, on a honeymoon on the Isle of Skye. Then they returned to live in a farm cottage on the outskirts of Steel's Pentlands constituency. Judy continued her work as a solicitor, and David his as Assistant Secretary of the Scottish Liberal party. They spent their evenings together – canvassing Pentlands voters.

The Steels threw themselves vigorously into building up the constituency's meagre organisation. On the face of it, Pentlands hardly seemed a winnable seat. The constituency had gone uncontested by the Liberals at the previous election, and when Steel became its prospective candidate there were fewer than one hundred members. But with post-Orpington optimism, Liberals everywhere felt anything might happen, and for a brief month the party led both Conservative and Labour in the opinion polls.

Since David's nomination as candidate, the Steels and a small band of dedicated helpers had systematically toured the constituency delivering leaflets advertising a series of meetings. As a result of this campaign, small audiences turned up to hear Steel expound on Liberal policies in draughty school halls. It hardly had the smell of a victory campaign about it, but at least it resulted in the tiny Pentlands Liberal party gathering new handfuls of members. It also produced a modest electoral success. In the 1962 local elections, one of Steel's hardest-working supporters, Robert Smith, who later became President of the Scottish Liberal party, won the Merchiston Ward. But all the other Liberal candidates, including Judy Steel who had been drafted in to make up the numbers, went down to defeat. Overall, the Liberals polled only about 15 per cent of the vote in the constituency – hardly an encouraging omen.

In an attempt to become better known among his constituents, Steel sent a steady stream of letters and press releases to the editors of local newspapers. These letters and early speeches reveal a mixture of traditional political rhetoric against the government of the day and some unusual practical suggestions.

For example, in an otherwise routine speech attacking the government's record on unemployment, Steel urged the government to build a new coal-fired power station in West Lothian to feed the national grid. He also called on the Coal Board in Scotland to establish a new research centre and coal processing plant for the manufacture of smokeless fuels. Steel added, 'While these two require government action, my third suggestion might be undertaken by either public or private enterprise. There is a wide potential for the creation of a large prefabricated-housing factory – not to produce more prefabs of the postwar type – but to exploit modern materials and designs, to offer a wide range of houses for private or local authority purchase. Imaginative and practical schemes of this kind could create in the immediate future a considerable number of jobs for Scotland.'

Steel was a serious and sober candidate, who had little truck with anything which smacked of extra-parliamentary action. He lambasted the Campaign for Nuclear Disarmament, the leading protest movement of its day. 'While not doubting the sincerity of their views, the CND contains too large a number of people who seem to think that a mixture of exhibitionism and nihilism is a substitute for political action,' Steel told a meeting at St Andrews University.

'I suggest to them that the general public is becoming rather tired of their demonstrations, particularly those ratepayers who will be called upon to foot the £4,000 bill for police measures taken at the recent demonstrations near the Holy Loch,' he added. Steel urged the CND to fight a parliamentary by-election in Scotland to 'reveal to the public the true measure of support which they have.'

Steel also continued a series of visits abroad which he had begun as a student, when he had visited the USSR, Poland and Switzerland. Denmark and Sweden were two of the countries on his new itinerary. In Denmark he met representatives of the main opposition party, and found out how in Denmark's multi-party state, politicians worked together in an ever-changing kaleidoscope of coalition governments. He returned from Denmark to tell his Pentlands constituents, 'The prestige of Britain abroad appears to me to have suffered a remarkable collapse over the past year.' The cause of this was, according to Steel, Prime Minister Harold Macmillan's handling of what had become known as the Profumo scandal.

Steel said, 'The security and other aspects of the Profumo affair have made us something of a laughing stock and there is a general amazement that the Prime Minister has not resigned. Politicians and political commentators may speculate on the advantage or damage to the Conservative party which Mr Macmillan's resignation would create, but as far as the standing of this country abroad is concerned there is unquestionably an urgent need for a new and younger face at the top as quickly as possible.'

The chance for a new, but not noticeably younger, face at the top came quicker than many, including Steel, had anticipated. Macmillan had been bothered by prostate trouble for some time, a fact which had been carefully concealed from most of his party. As he prepared to travel to the Conservative party conference in Blackpool in October 1963, the condition worsened seriously, and Macmillan's doctors advised that immediate surgery was required. Macmillan had planned to announce to the Conservative conference, in his traditional end of conference address to the assembled delegates, his intention to retire in the New Year. But his unceremonious hospitalisation threw the Conservative party into confusion. In the unseemly scramble up the greasy pole which followed Macmillan's untimely departure several political careers, including R. A. Butler's, came to an end. And Lord Home, previously Foreign Secretary, emerged as leader of the Conservative party.

Once again, the paths of Steel and the Douglas Home family crossed. The emergence of Home played a key part in Steel's early political success. The tweedy, feudal, grouse-shooting image of the new Tory leader, so out of tune with the white heat of the technological revolution which Harold Wilson proclaimed in the early 1960s, created just the right political conditions for Steel to win his Roxburgh, Selkirk and Peebles constituency in 1965. The fact that the constituency was on Sir Alec's doorstep, a stone's throw from the family seat of the Hirsel in Berwickshire, finally convinced many Conservatives, including probably Sir Alec himself, that if the Tories could not win that kind of constituency, their hopes of winning the next election were about as realistic as a grouse's chance of survival on the Glorious Twelfth.

However, the immediate problem was to find a constituency for Sir Alec to represent. The appointment of Sir Alec, a Member of the House of Lords, as leader of the Conservative party had created a constitutional furore. No Prime Minister had sat in the Lords since Lord Salisbury at the end of the nineteenth century. It was a well-established constitutional convention that the Prime Minister should lead from the Commons. So, for Sir Alec, a transfer from the aristocratic red leather benches of the Lords to the more plebeian green leather of the Commons, became a matter of some urgency. Sir Alec hoped to achieve this by fighting a by-election in the true-blue Highland constituency of Kinross and West Perthshire, which, it was reasonably assumed, he would win without too much difficulty.

This important by-election gave Steel his first chance of being at the centre of a nationally important political event. The fact that a serving Prime Minister had to fight a parliamentary by-election in order to secure a seat in the Commons was a highly unusual, if not unique, event in British politics. As such, it attracted international attention from the world's press.

During the campaign, the Liberal candidate, Alistair Duncan Millar, a local laird and a son of a former Liberal MP, emerged as the main challenger to Sir Alec. He actually came second on polling day. The Scottish Liberal party had originally decided that their General Secretary Arthur Purdom should take charge of the management of the campaign. Part of the way through, however, Purdom fell ill, and Steel was drafted in to take over.

This was something of a daunting task, for Steel had not run a parliamentary election campaign before, nor had he been on the party's training course for political agents. However, he had helped out at a number of earlier by-election campaigns, and now set about organising a string of public meetings, canvassing and other activities around the villages and hamlets of the sprawling constituency. He had got to know something about how the press worked during his days at university, and as President of the Student Representative Council had frequently been quoted in Scottish newspapers, especially during the Grimond rectorial installation. Now he put this knowledge to use in organising daily press conferences for his candidate. With world interest in the constituency, the number of journalists attending the morning press conferences frequently exceeded the audience of dour Highlanders who turned out for the evening political meetings. Over the years, Steel has established generally good relationships with a large number of working journalists. Many of his contacts with the well-known names of Fleet Street date from this parliamentary by-election.

Sir Alec duly won the by-election and entered the House of Commons towards the end of 1963. Steel returned to his work as Assistant Secretary to the Scottish Liberal party. During the remainder of 1963 and through most of 1964, the position of the Conservative party in the opinion polls improved from the low levels to which it had sunk in the middle of 1962. As the Tory party crept up the polls, the Liberal tide, which had reached a flood at the time of Orpington in March 1962, receded.

Steel noted this with some concern. His short period at the Scottish Liberal party had already given him time to think about the strategic implications of the Liberal party's position. And he already believed there was little point in Liberal candidates fighting constituencies where they had a minimal chance of success and where they were likely to poll poorly. The development of this thinking has been especially important in Steel's approach to Liberal party politics in subsequent years.

As a hard-headed realist, Steel has never believed that the Liberal party will sweep into power on a sudden wave of popular support generated overnight. He does believe that the party has an important role to play in British politics in bringing together progressive non-socialist forces, and that Liberals could well share power in some form of government created by this process.

In this, he has followed and developed Jo Grimond's ideas about radical realignment.

Throughout Steel's twenty years in active party politics, the prospects for radical realignment have looked alternately rosy and bleak. They were bleak in 1963, rosy in 1964 when Labour won the general election with a paper-thin majority, and bleak again when Labour increased its majority at the 1966 general election. However, consistently through his political career, Steel has maintained that Liberals need to work with other like-minded people to achieve their objectives, and that political labels, such as Liberal or Labour are less important than shared beliefs. It follows from this that Steel does not necessarily believe the Liberal party needs to fight every seat at every election, like the Labour and Conservative parties, and that in some cases Liberals can be more effective by not fighting every seat. Although Steel had taken on board the theoretical basis of Grimond's ideas for a radical realignment of British politics whilst still a student at university, it was while working for the Scottish Liberal party that he became aware of the important practical implications of this approach. That the party would not fight every seat and that the party should not fight those seats in which its vote was likely to underline its weakness rather than its strength were among these implications. Steel put these views in writing after helping to organise a disastrous by-election campaign for the Liberals in Dumfries in December 1963. The Liberal candidate lost his deposit. 'These six words,' Steel wrote in the party's newspaper, *Liberal News*, 'do the Liberal cause more damage than any six sentences uttered by Tory or Labour propagandists.'

Steel argued that constituencies should only put up candidates where they could fight a reasonable campaign. And he wrote, 'I am always alarmed when I read of candidates and others in responsible positions urging that the party should adopt yet more candidates and fight on a yet broader front to return a Liberal government at the next election.

'To my mind this is an invitation to mass suicide, and it is to be hoped that there will be no further adoptions except in those constituencies where there is a good organisation already operating, and which have been seeking a candidate for some time. I am even dubious of the worth of the statement often heard hitherto that we are putting up enough candidates to form a

Liberal government should the public wish it.

'The reason for this statement is, I take it, that many people will not vote Liberal because we are at present unable to form a government. But people don't analyse the number of Liberal candidates when declaring that we cannot yet form a government – they merely apply common sense.'

Steel urged that the Liberal long-term aim should be to form a government, and that the next government would be influenced by the size of the Liberal vote in the country and the effectiveness of Liberal representation in the Commons. He added, 'Liberals must be people who are known to exist and to be active, and not strange creatures who arrive seeking votes during an election, like missionaries with a new gospel from an unknown land.'

This was unconventional thinking for the Liberal party, many of whose members nursed a secret hope that the party could miraculously be swept to power on a wave of protest at the failures of the other two parties. Nor was Steel's demand, made in the same article, that the thirty Liberal candidates most likely to lose their deposits at the next election be 'weeded out now', likely to endear him to most party members.

Although Steel was still largely unknown in the Liberal party – certainly outside Scotland – this was a new brand of tough talking which was bound to attract attention.

4

Into Parliament

For David Steel, Roxburgh, Selkirk and Peebles is more than a parliamentary constituency. It is also home − a haven from the rough political world of Westminster. Home for Steel is a small house, converted from three adjacent cottages, in the one-street hamlet of Ettrick Bridge, Selkirkshire.

Steel shares this modest home with wife, Judy; sons, Graeme and Rory; a daughter, Catriona; adopted son, Billy; a cat; and an apparently ferocious black Labrador called Jill, obtained on police security recommendation. Outside is a 'very ordinary horse' called Hamlet, and a collection of chickens. Cherrydene, the Steel residence, stands at the end of a picturesque street, opposite the village pub, the Cross Keys. Ettrick Bridge, like many other similar towns and villages in the Borders, stands for the kind of qualities Steel exemplifies − 'old-fashioned things like modesty, politeness and incredibly hard work,' *Daily Mail* columnist Anne Batt called them.

Yet Steel is no born Borderer. He had no connection with the area until his adoption as its Liberal candidate in 1964. But in the intervening years the Borders have become identified with him, and he with the Borders. So much so that he can authentically claim in his election literature to be the 'voice of the Borders'. With a majority which has climbed over the years to more than 11,000, Steel can confidently look forward to lifelong tenure of his Roxburgh, Selkirk and Peebles seat in Parliament − for the Borderer is a man of tenacious loyalty.

Much of the Steel story takes place in this Roxburgh, Selkirk and Peebles constituency, surely one of the loveliest in the country. For it is to this constituency, perhaps even more than to the Liberal party, that Steel owes his first loyalty. At the same time, his success in winning and holding Roxburgh, Selkirk and Peebles is a mini case-study in the kind of radical realignment which Steel wants to see in the rest of the country. The constituency is one in which only two parties really matter now – Liberal and Conservative. The Labour vote has been whittled down over the years to deposit-losing level.

So what kind of constituency is Roxburgh, Selkirk and Peebles? It is, perhaps, an unusual constituency in which to find a strong radical tradition. Roxburgh, Selkirk and Peebles stretches over 1,288 square miles of southern Scotland, from the 'raddled braes of industrial Lanarkshire to the Cheviots and the lower reaches of the river Tweed'. It is a country of hills and valleys, with an agricultural industry based on sheep farming, stock raising, and upland farms. However, the majority of the working population gain their livelihood from some form of non-agricultural industry. For this is one of the great textile areas of Britain. Although, like the textile industry in other parts of Britain, it has been hit by recession and cheap imports, the high quality, specialised woollen garments produced in the mills of towns like Galashiels, Hawick and Innerleithen have been better able to resist foreign competition. In recent years, Borders industry, stimulated by the Scottish Development Agency, has diversified into chemicals, electronics and local crafts. Even in hard times, the Borders remains one of the most prosperous parts of Scotland.

Politically speaking, the constituency has been Conservative for most of this century. From 1923 to 1950, it was the family seat of the Dukes of Buccleuch. Roxburgh, Selkirk and Peebles is a real land of the lairds. The valleys abound with castles and stately homes, the family residences of noble Scottish families. Three dukes have their ancestral homes in the Borders – Buccleuch, Roxburgh and Sutherland – one marquis – Lothian – and at least three earls – Dalkeith, Minto, Haig. In addition, there are enough retired military to start another Scottish uprising. Despite this, Liberalism has always had a strong hold on the hearts of the common folk of the Scottish Borders. The Roxburgh and Selkirk constituency elected Archie Macdonald, a local businessman, as its Liberal MP in 1950. But he lost his seat in the next general election a year later, when the county of Peeblesshire was added to the constituency, and the Conservative majority climbed throughout the 1950s.

The story of how Steel became the Liberal candidate for Roxburgh, Selkirk and Peebles is a classic case of how success

46

often depends on being in the right place at the right time. As we have seen, Steel had been adopted for the Edinburgh Pentlands constituency, a hopeless Liberal prospect, in October 1961. His energy in building up the local Liberal Association had been greatly admired by the top men of the Scottish Liberal party. But as far as finding Steel a safe Liberal seat was concerned, well, he was still young and had to prove his mettle at the polls – and anyway, outside Jo Grimond's Orkney and Shetland constituency, there were no safe Liberal seats in Scotland, and Jo had no intention of standing down.

In fact, Steel faced the gloomy prospect of ten or more years ploughing a lonely furrow in near hopeless seats before getting the chance at a constituency which was even half-winnable. So he gritted his teeth and continued to pound the streets of Pentlands.

Meanwhile, down in Roxburgh, Selkirk and Peebles, there was rebellion afoot in the burghs. Following the 1959 general election, at which the Conservative MP, Commander Charles Donaldson, had increased his majority to more than 9,000, the local Liberal Association had adopted a new candidate, the Honourable James Tennant. Tennant, a merchant banker and son of one of the biggest landowners in the Borders, seemed like a natural to appeal to a constituency stuffed with dukes and earls. Tennant had all the right Liberal connections. He was related to Margot Asquith, wife of the Liberal Prime Minister. This meant he also had a family connection with Jo Grimond, for Grimond had married Asquith's grand-daughter.

Despite these impeccable Liberal credentials, the local party members were dissatisfied with their candidate. Although considered a knowledgeable and kindly man, it was felt by the leading Liberals in the constituency that he did not have the common touch or sense of occasion needed in a constituency where the Liberal vote was essentially a working-class vote. One local member recalls how he harangued her in her kitchen about the intricacies of world finance, while she prepared her husband's supper. This kind of behaviour led to a crisis of confidence in the Association, and Tennant resigned in 1963, without fighting an election, leaving the Border Liberals without a candidate.

With the possibility of a general election only months away, Roxburgh Liberals needed a candidate fast. Jo Grimond prowled round the Scottish Liberals' headquarters in Edinburgh com-

47

plaining that one of the most promising seats in Scotland had no candidate. Nor were the Borders Liberals having any luck in hooking the kind of big fish candidate they felt they deserved. Their first choice, Derek Starforth, Joint Honorary Treasurer of the Scottish Liberal party, turned them down. He was already committed to fight at East Renfrewshire. Another possibility, former colonial officer John Matthew, politely declined. He had just been appointed Assistant Bursar of Winchester College – too far away to nurse the constituency effectively.

That autumn Steel turned up to address the annual general meeting of Roxburgh, Selkirk and Peebles Liberals. As Assistant Secretary of the Scottish Liberal party, he had been booked as a guest speaker. The man who chaired the meeting that night, the remarkably named Riddle Dumble, recalls: 'We cleared up the normal business of the meeting and then I asked him to speak. And immediately I know my own reaction was: this chap knows his stuff.'

Dumble, who later became Steel's election agent in 1970 says, 'He was very good and could deal with all the questions, even though he was a young chap. We all agreed this was the sort of bloke we could do with as candidate.'

The Borderers brushed over Steel's youthfulness – he looked even younger than his twenty-five years. 'If he's guid enough, he's old enough,' intoned one ageing local supporter.

Faced with an invitation to move to the Borders, Steel had only a moment's hesitation before telling his Pentland's Association he was leaving. They accepted the inevitable, with varying degrees of bad grace, at a stormy meeting presided over by George Mackie, chairman of the Scottish Liberal party's organisation committee. The *Liberal News'* headline on the story read 'SLP's bright boy swops divisions'. Later, Mackie had a vote of censure passed on him by the Scottish Liberals' Executive Committee for aiding Steel's defection. Mackie and Steel became great friends, and in the 1979 general election Lord Mackie acted as a surrogate campaigner in Roxburgh, Selkirk and Peebles while Steel toured the country as party leader.

At this point, the influence of the Homes once again asserted itself on Steel's political career. Sir Alec had become Prime Minister in October 1963. Everyone assumed he would call an election in the spring of 1964. Instead, early in the New Year, Sir

Alec announced that he intended to remain at Number 10 until the autumn. This was vitally important for Steel, because it meant that, instead of having to fight a new constituency within a few weeks and with a minimum of preparation, he had several months to establish himself.

Steel was formally adopted as prospective parliamentary Liberal candidate for Roxburgh, Selkirk and Peebles in January 1964. By May, he had quit his Edinburgh home and moved to a cottage just outside Galashiels. The cottage had been provided by Christopher Scott, a local landowner and Liberal supporter. Steel's wife, Judy, later gave up her job as an Edinburgh solicitor in order to help her husband with the campaign.

The Steels faced a daunting task. Although the seat had Liberal traditions, the Conservative majority had grown to nearly 10,000 and the sitting Member, Commander Charles Donaldson, who had first gained the seat from the Liberals in 1951, looked well entrenched. Donaldson, a former Canadian naval officer, was reckoned to be well liked by his constituents, although his parliamentary career had been undistinguished. He had been Parliamentary Private Secretary to the Lord Advocate from 1954 to 1959, hardly an exalted position.

Nevertheless, Steel believed Donaldson would be a hard man to beat. Realistically, he recognised he could not expect to achieve it in one go. With what some thought was stunning cheek, he had demanded from the Roxburgh Selection Committee the right to fight the constituency at three successive elections. The Association, which had had the stuffing knocked out of it by successive defeats, meekly agreed.

Now adopted, Steel demanded that the chairman, a retired colonel, should retire from office. Steel felt the colonel was out of touch with local political feeling, and was running the Association too much like a military organisation. The mostly working-class party members – whose sympathies were with the 'other ranks' – objected to the colonel's high-handed attitude. Steel realised that the local Liberal party would have to become a more aggressive campaigning organisation if he were to win the seat. An elderly lady party worker who referred disparagingly to a new member convert from the Tories as a 'turncoat' was sharply reminded by Steel that if he was to win the constituency they would have to find another 5,000 turncoats.

Steel's campaign tactic was to become immersed in the life of the Borders so that the fiercely proud Borderers could consider him one of them. He became a Moss Trooper, a local distinction awarded to those who complete a gruelling twenty-five-mile cross-country horse ride from Hawick to Mosspaul and back. He became a familiar figure at the division's Liberal clubs. These have always played an important part in the success of Border Liberalism. Their combined membership is several thousand and they provide a natural rallying point for Liberals.

During the summer of 1964, the Steels embarked on an exhaustive tour of the towns and villages of the sprawling constituency. Many political commentators, with their opinion polls and swingometers, fail to appreciate the importance of a personality in rural campaigning. The received wisdom of politics is that the candidate can never make more than 2 or 3 per cent difference to a party's result in a given constituency. This is a theory devised by people who live in cities. It is not true in rural communities, particularly in a constituency like Roxburgh, Selkirk and Peebles, where the large distances between communities and the geography of the area make each town or village rather insular in outlook. In rural campaigning, a word-of-mouth recommendation can be as important as a supportive newspaper editorial or a party political broadcast. In short, in the kind of constituency which Steel has, the candidate *is* important.

Steel recognised this from the moment he went to the Borders. And his summer tour was designed to make him better known in every town, village and hamlet of the constituency. In each village, Steel made at least three stops – at the post office, the school teacher and the parish minister. He reckoned that even if he was not able to meet anyone else, these three local worthies would talk about him to other villagers.

In addition to this, Riddle Dumble, who replaced the sacked colonel as constituency chairman, organised scores of political and social functions for Steel to attend. Dumble recalls that in the months before the Steels moved to Galashiels, Steel would drive down from Edinburgh in the late afternoon to have tea at his home before going on to a meeting or other function.

Dumble says, 'He never refused anything. We got him round all the Liberal branches very quickly. Of course, he is a very pleasant person to meet and was immediately well received by everybody. It was amazing, actually, how well he was received by the normally reticent Borderers. I think part of the reason was he was prepared to stop and listen to people.' Steel's active involvement in the constituency contrasted well with Donaldson's rather arm's-length approach to his seat.

Yet when the election came, the scratchy Liberal organisation hardly compared to the Tories' smooth election machine, which had nearly 10,000 paid-up members organised in eighty-three branches. The Steels spent much of their time organising the nuts and bolts of the campaign, such as booking halls for meetings, arranging newspaper advertisements and putting up posters. The Liberals did not even have a proper headquarters. The whole campaign was run from the front room of a member's home.

In spite of these difficulties, Steel managed to carry the Liberal campaign to most parts of the constituency, addressing two or three public meetings a night. Roxburgh, Selkirk and Peebles is one of the few constituencies in the country where public meetings are still an important part of a political campaign. In 1964 Steel could expect to get an audience of sixty or seventy to a meeting in a small village, and between two hundred and three hundred in a larger town. And these audiences turned up without any outside big-name speaker to attract them. The importance of public meetings has been a feature of Steel's electoral success. Steel is at his best when addressing a smallish audience (up to a few hundred) in homely surroundings, like the village halls and parish rooms of his constituency. In these circumstances he is able to develop a close rapport with an audience, and much of the stiffness of his larger, more formal appearances, such as at Liberal conferences when he reads from a written text, disappears. He does, in fact, prefer to speak extempore from brief notes, and also excels in the cut and thrust of question time.

In other ways, Steel showed himself to be an innovative campaigner in his first parliamentary election contest. He produced more and better leaflets than Borders Liberals had been used to, and insisted on sending an election address to every elector, rather than to every house as most candidates do. Steel correctly believed that political loyalties are split in more families than opinion polls suggest. He also introduced lapel buttons, which other parties copied in later campaigns.

Steel fought his campaign largely on local issues, like many other successful Liberal campaigners. He argued that the Borders' needs had been ignored in Scotland. He pointed to the need for a new Borders hospital, and criticised Donaldson for voting in favour of the Beeching Report on British Railways, which threatened the local railway line with closure.

On polling day, Steel found he had failed to unseat Donaldson by 1,739 votes. Yet he had reason to be satisfied with his result. His 17,185 votes was the highest individual Liberal vote in Scotland, and he had substantially reduced the Conservative majority. Moreover, as Harold Wilson's newly elected Labour government had an overall parliamentary majority of only five, it could scarcely last its full term. Another general election must surely come within two years.

However, the election left Steel with a problem. He now had no job. His contract as Assistant Secretary of the Scottish Liberal party had expired on polling day. And the impoverished Scottish Liberals, with funds depleted by the election, could not afford to re-employ him full-time at his former salary. During his time with the SLP, he had made some contacts with BBC Scotland, and the Beeb now offered him a six-month contract as a reporter/presenter on a regional current affairs programme. However, Steel hardly had time to find his feet in this job.

He was recording his programme in the BBC studios in Glasgow in December 1964, when a colleague came in to tell him that Donaldson had died and there would be a by-election in Roxburgh, Selkirk and Peebles. At first, Steel thought it was a tasteless practical joke, but a copy of the telex tape confirmed the news. At once, the BBC suspended Steel from further broadcasting. He reacted angrily by pointing out that he had not been adopted as the prospective parliamentary Liberal candidate in his constituency. This was true, even though Steel had reached a secret agreement with his local party bosses that he would be available for the next election when it came, and he persuaded them that for a few months it would be more valuable for him to be seen by his constituents on their television screens than on their doorsteps.

Arthur Purdom, Steel's former boss at the Scottish Liberal party, dubbed the Steel telly ban as 'irrelevant' because the Roxburgh by-election had not yet begun. Purdom pointed out that Geoffrey Johnson Smith, another broadcaster-politician, who was standing for the Conservatives at a by-election in East Grinstead, had been allowed on the screen. The Beeb's ban stayed – but Steel was paid up to the end of his contract. This incident led to a rift between Steel and the BBC which lasted for several years. It was only healed when Steel presented a *Songs of Praise* programme from his father's church, St Michael's, Linlithgow, in 1970, and was promptly signed up to present others transmitted from Scottish churches over the next three years.

Steel had not expected to be fighting the Borders seat again so soon, but he had been preparing for a new campaign. The general election had produced sweeping Liberal gains in the Highlands, where Liberal candidates campaigned on the need for a positive government programme to regenerate the area. Steel recognised a similarity between the situation in the Highlands and his own constituency. The Borders had suffered over the preceding two decades from depopulation. In the previous ten years, something like 8,000 people had left the Borders. This included about a quarter of all the young people aged between twenty and forty-five. Steel believed this trend had to be halted, not only for the good of the Borders but the whole country. Depopulation in the Borders leads to overcrowding in cities like London, and resulting evils such as Rachmanism.

Early in 1965, Steel set out his views on this problem in a pamphlet called *Boost for the Borders*. This argued that a development authority should be set up to tackle the depopulation problem. The authority should consist of three men, 'not retired admirals, diplomats or trade unionists, but men in the prime of life, to work full time on the task of regenerating the Borders.' At least one should be a Borderer, and the authority should work to a ten-year plan.

Steel said, 'We feel that the problem of depopulation should be tackled with the same energy and vigour as unemployment and we are not satisfied that the other parties have paid enough attention to the parts of our country which are declining, such as the Highlands and Borders. The Borders is an area which requires drastic action now.' Steel's Border authority would have 'considerable powers' and capital funds and would be able to advise the Scottish Secretary on public expenditure – for example, on roads and hospitals – and 'at the same time promote private enterprise by giving credit facilities to industrial, tourist or agricultural schemes designed to produce more employment.'

Every successful campaigner needs a *cause célèbre*, and depopulation became Steel's cause and the major issue of the by-election campaign. The Tories bungled the issue by asserting that Steel's talk of depopulation was hysterical nonsense. The ebullient, moustacheod MP Gerald Nabarro breezed into the constituency and declared that talk of Borders depopulation was 'ballyhoo'. He based this on the fact that the peer of the realm with whom he stayed during his visit had increased the number of servants he kept. 'Now we know the Tory answer to depopulation,' Steel told his delighted audiences. 'Everyone should hire more servants.'

The Roxburgh by-election of 1965 was fought in a blaze of national publicity. Steel believed that in order to win he would have to persuade some of the 7,007 people who voted Labour at the general election to switch to him – a practical application of the policy of radical realignment. But he reckoned this could be difficult, for Labour fielded the same candidate as at the general election, a likeable and articulate lawyer from Edinburgh, Ronald King Murray.

The Tories chose Robin McEwen, son of the late Sir John McEwen, of Marchmont, Berwickshire. McEwen, an identikit Tory – he had been at Eton, Oxford and in the Brigade of Guards – was, however, a true Borderer, and on the face of it a strong candidate. Steel later described him as 'agreeable and able'.

However, McEwen's patrician manner at public meetings rattled voters. He easily lost his temper when provoked by hostile questions. When they found out about this, Liberals organised teams of hecklers to visit Tory meetings and provoke him to fits of rage. Members of the Tory shadow cabinet, who poured into the Borders during the campaign, would sit beside McEwen on the platform at meetings, their heads buried in their hands, as an angry McEwen berated an over-zealous questioner. Even the performance of special campaign songs by McEwen's folk-singing brothers, Rory and Alex, could not soothe the atmosphere. Liberals dubbed the Tory meetings 'two singers and a comedian'.

The Tories should have decreased the importance of public meetings in their campaign. Instead, the presence of Tory star turns like Sir Keith Joseph, Edward Heath and Quintin Hogg, boosted meeting attendances to record levels. Steel correctly predicted that the presence of so many Tory 'big guns' could backfire on the Conservative campaign. He pointed out in speeches that James II of Scotland, 'James of the fiery face', was killed while laying siege to Roxburgh Castle in 1460 by the bursting of his own largest cannon – an intriguing historical analogy.

The Liberals sent their big guns as well. Jo Grimond addressed huge meetings in Galashiels, Kelso and Jedburgh. Orpington by-election victor Eric Lubbock (now Lord Avebury) visited the constituency to confirm that the scent of a Liberal win was in the air. Jeremy Thorpe also spent several days in the constituency, and for the first time came to know and respect Steel as a young Liberal politician. Thorpe spent polling day driving Steel round the constituency. He had no doubt why Steel would win. 'The candidate must be credible, not only in that he has a chance of winning but that, if he does so, he understands the problems of the division and has the capacity to do something about them,' he said.

At 2.00 a.m. on 25 March 1965, Steel appeared on the steps of Jedburgh Town Hall with the Returning Officer and the other candidates. His wife Judy smiled at his side as the result was announced:

Steel (Liberal)	21,549
McEwen (Conservative)	16,942
King Murray (Labour)	4,936
Kerr (Independent Scottish Nationalist)	411

Steel's 4,607 majority exceeded even his expectations. A deep-throated roar of approval from the crowd gathered round the town hall steps greeted the result. Liberals cracked open the whisky and carried Steel through the streets of Jedburgh, while a crowd of four hundred supporters roared out the victory songs.

At twenty-six, and at his second attempt, Steel had been elected as the youngest Member of the House of Commons. Steel's victory was tinged with sadness. His paternal grandfather died on polling day, but the news was kept from him until the day was over.

5

Life as an MP

Steel awoke from a few hours' sleep after his by-election victory
to find the result the subject of intense speculation. Two big
questions dominated the newspaper headlines. Could Sir Alec
Douglas Home, the Tory leader, weather this blow to his
leadership, a blow delivered on his very Borders doorstep? And
did the obvious switch of voters from the forlorn Labour
candidate to the victorious Liberal mark the start of a spontaneous
radical realignment among voters?

Steel had his own answer to the first question. 'If the theme of a
Border candidate backing a Border Tory leader does not go down
well in the Borders, I don't know where it does. I suppose Sir
Alec could say that all the contenders for leadership played a part
in this campaign and failed. He stayed out of it, but it gives him
cold comfort.' Whisperings of dissatisfaction about Sir Alec's
leadership of the Conservative party increased noticeably after
this result, and he finally quit four months later on 22 July.

Far more important, were the questions raised about radical
realignment. Steel's views on this subject have remained
remarkably consistent over the years, from his early days at
university, when Jo Grimond's attractive espousal of the case for
a radical, non-socialist alternative to the Conservative party
brought Steel into the Liberal party, to his suggested alliance with
the Social Democratic party.

As far as the switch of Labour votes to the Liberal candidate in
the by-election was concerned, the result was inconclusive. Steel
had actively campaigned to win more votes from Labour, and
their poll had slipped about 4 per cent to a deposit-losing level.
But the Tory poll had slipped 4 per cent as well and, in fact, Steel
would have won his seat – albeit on a much narrower margin –
just on the swing of votes from Conservative to Liberal. So in the
short term, the case for realignment was not proven. In the longer
term, Steel pointed out that Labour's share of the poll had fallen

by half since the 1959 general election, and had resulted in the election of a Liberal MP. He had no doubt that he owed his election to a radical realignment of voters working at a local level.

The effect of this on Steel's whole political outlook should not be underestimated. He starts from the view that radical realignment is, *per se*, desirable. So do most Liberal MPs. But most Liberal MPs owe their election to Conservative voters switching to the Liberals. As a result, these MPs must constantly look over their shoulders to make sure their action and policies do not offend their erstwhile-Tory patrons. Steel has always believed that he has not been in this position, and so there has never been a hint of circumspection in his drive for a realignment of radical political forces. As we shall see, this general political view has been reinforced during Steel's political career by his success in working with politicians of other parties in cross-party campaigns to achieve specific reforms.

In the months immediately following Steel's election, radical realignment became an important topic of political discussion, especially in the Liberal party. This was not so much a result of the Liberals' efforts to promote the idea, as of the fact that the Labour government teetered on a knife-edge majority of three votes in the House of Commons. During the spring and summer of 1965, Jo Grimond floated, at first vaguely and later more specifically, the idea of a formal arrangement with the Labour government. Two weeks before the Roxburgh by-election, Grimond had said in *The Times* that the Liberals wanted a long-range agreement with the government or a general election. 'We must have an agreement for a few months on some purpose we both want,' he said.

In June Grimond set out his views in more detail in newspaper interviews and a party political broadcast. He made it clear that he was not offering Labour any formal deal, but merely setting out his views in general terms. But he forcefully argued that the terms of any deal between Labour and the Liberals should be worked out *before* Labour lost its majority in the House, and should be a comprehensive, not an *ad hoc*, arrangement. Before setting out these views, Grimond consulted his parliamentary party – now up to double figures after Steel's election. Only Steel and Jeremy Thorpe positively endorsed the Grimond view, the majority of the parliamentary party offering grudging acquiescence. Interestingly, history repeated itself when Steel led the Liberals into the Lib-Lab pact with James Callaghan's government in 1967. Steel advanced similar arguments to Grimond to justify the arrangement, and found most of his parliamentary party, including Grimond, only acquiescing in the arrangement.

In support of the proposed Grimond pact, Steel argued that it was no use Labour expecting the Liberals to support the government in the hope of its passing a few Liberal-backed measures. In a controversial article in the *New Statesman* he said, 'We cannot be expected to stomach a mass of bad Toryism and some irrelevant pieces of socialist doctrine in order to gain a few morsels of good radical legislation.' Steel wanted a formal deal between the two parties to recognise that an agreed package of policies would be needed.

Wilson ignored the Liberal overtures, but the voters still showed some desire for a realignment. In by-elections, voters switched to Liberal candidates in those seats where the party was in a strong position to win. Where Labour was in a strong position, the Liberal vote fell sharply. Steel questioned whether this was such a bad thing if it led to the realignment the party was seeking. 'We cannot complain about Liberal voters deserting a candidate who had no chance of winning at Hull and voting Labour, thus causing a Liberal lost deposit,' he said after one by-election, 'if at the same time we welcome Labour voters deserting their fold and causing lost deposits at Roxburgh, Orpington and North Devon in order to return Liberal MPs in place of Tories.'

This was just the kind of talk designed to enrage Liberal workers in the majority of contituencies where Liberals had little hope of success. Yet Steel had never felt it was worth pretending the Liberals were somehow going to sweep the country miraculously. He took — and takes — the pragmatic view that Liberals should seek power by working with like-minded individuals. During the brief period from Steel's entry into Parliament until the 1966 general election, when it tantalizingly seemed that the Liberals might hold the parliamentary balance of power, Steel's views on the strategy and tactics of working towards a practical realignment of radical MPs in Parliament developed significantly. The lessons he learnt during this period were useful when he led the Liberal party into its arrangement with the Labour government in 1967.

In fact, Steel learnt a great deal from this period in Parliament, and began to establish himself as an effective parliamentarian. Yet the Steel who took his seat in the Commons on 30 March 1965 – the day before his twenty-seventh birthday – was far less green than many new Members, certainly than the Members in his age bracket. Steel's experience in university politics had equipped him as an effective speaker and a nimble debater. His period at the Scottish Liberal party provided experience of dealing with political journalists, and his brief spell at the BBC had turned a natural aptitude for television into an engaging TV personality.

So the Steel who marched up to the Bar of the House, flanked on each side by his sponsors, George Mackie and Eric Lubbock, to take the oath of office was already well equipped as a professional politician. Labour and Tory Members gawped at the callow youth who took his seat confidently on the Liberal bench. He looked hardly old enough to have left school, let alone to have been elected to Parliament. His wife and mother and father gazed on proudly from the Strangers' Gallery.

Steel wasted no time in getting down to parliamentary business. He slapped down a question to the Minister of Transport on the future of the Edinburgh–Hawick–Carlisle railway which ran through his constituency. Then he marched off to vote in a routine division on the postal services.

On his second day he faced his first real political crisis of conscience. Parliament debated a measure to retain the death penalty for murderers killing a second time. Opinion polls had conclusively demonstrated that this measure had huge popular support among the population at large, and presumably among Steel's constituents as well. When these tricky emotional issues crop up in Parliament, many Members find it convenient to be called away on pressing business elsewhere. Not Steel. Throughout his political career, on a wide range of issues of conscience, and on some unpopular political issues, Steel has not been afraid to take a stand. He voted against retaining the death penalty.

Steel waited about two weeks before making his maiden speech. This is quick for a new Member, but slow for a new Liberal Member. Cyril Smith, the burly MP for Rochdale, made his within two hours of taking his seat. Steel spoke in a debate on the budget and the economic situation. It enabled him to raise the subject which had been the major theme of his campaign, depopulation in the Borders. Steel criticised the government for using the yardstick of unemployment to decide whether an area warranted designation as a development area. 'We in the Borders have no unemployment on a very large scale and do not qualify as a development district. We have been constantly passed over and yet we have this tremendous drain of population year by year. I consider that depopulation is nothing more than exported unemployment,' Steel said. He demanded that the government consider regional variations in taxation to help depressed areas.

To become a Member of Parliament means a change in anyone's life style. And this is especially true of Liberal MPs, who suffer much greater pressures than Members from other parties. For a start, Steel joined a tiny parliamentary party raised to ten Members by his by-election win – the first time the parliamentary Liberal party had been in double figures since 1950. The Liberal party is usually about one-thirtieth of the size of the Labour and Conservative parties, yet it tries to play a full role in the work of the House. This means that every member of the parliamentary party has to have a 'front-bench' job, and sometimes two or three. Steel became the Liberals' parliamentary spokesman on employment matters as soon as he entered the House, shadowing Ray Gunter, a wily old campaigner, who was Minister of Labour.

For Steel, this was very much a case of drawing the short straw. All the jobs he might have liked had been taken, so he had to make do with what was available. Employment legislation was far removed from Steel's main political interests, such as foreign and Commonwealth affairs, and from the main concerns of his Border constituents. Yet he managed to find a few occasions to make some routine plugs for the traditional Liberal case for more co-partnership in industry. At September's Liberal assembly, at which he received a rousing reception from delegates, he called for the introduction of industrial partnership schemes into nationalised industries. He also wanted tax incentives to encourage private industry to bring in partnership schemes.

Steel did not sparkle with original ideas about employment, but he could hardly be expected to. Liberal MPs do not have large battalions of researchers at their party's headquarters to help them develop policy proposals. The Liberal party's research department consists of three harassed researchers and one secretary. They are expected to brief Liberal MPs on the issues of the day, prepare party publications and answer a never-ending stream of enquiries from the public about Liberal policy on almost every subject from nuclear power to Cornish mackerel fishing.

Liberal MPs also find they have much heavier postbags, on the whole, than their Labour or Tory counterparts. Partly this is the result of representing mostly rural constituencies where the Member of Parliament is more well known than in an anonymous urban area, and is thought of as a natural person to turn to for advice or information. In part, it is the result of Liberal MPs fighting active community-based campaigns, which raise compelling local issues, in order to win their seats. Liberal MPs also find they get letters from Liberal voters in other constituencies who do not trust their own Labour or Tory Members to deal with a grievance effectively. Steel had a heavy postbag right from the start of his political career, and, as a result of this, had to hire a secretary straight away. Many new Members manage by sharing a secretary for the first years of their parliamentary career.

Liberal MPs are also expected to trail round the country trying to whip up enthusiasm amongst forlorn bands of sympathisers in hopeless constituencies. Steel has never had much taste for this activity, and keeps it to a minimum. During his first spell in Parliament, he had a ready-made excuse for refusing the hundreds of invitations which poured in. His 4,607 majority was far from impregnable, and with the next general election perhaps only months away he had to devote the maximum attention to his own political backyard in the Borders.

Steel slipped easily, although not comfortably, into the life of a new MP. In this, he was lucky to have the support of his wife, Judy, who has solidly backed him throughout his political career. While Parliament was sitting, Steel's political week began early Monday morning. He rose, and left Abbotsferry Cottage at Boleside near Galashiels for the drive to Edinburgh's Turnhouse Airport. He took a plane south, and a tube to the House of Commons, arriving about noon to a long political day of House of Commons work – meetings, correspondence, preparing speeches and more meetings. Rarely did he leave the House before ten or eleven at night to return to the National Liberal Club, the Gothic monstrosity on the Embankment, which became Steel's London base during his first few years in Parliament. Steel had rejected the idea of having a plush flat in the division-bell area of Westminster, and in any case he could not afford one.

The Tuesday to Thursday routine became one of working at the House of Commons from mid-morning until late at night. Most Thursdays Steel would try to catch the late plane back to Edinburgh, and arrive at Edinburgh at two o'clock in the morning, climb into an ageing 1959 Humber car and drive forty miles home to Boleside. On the seat beside him would be a suitcase containing his week's dirty washing for laundering during the following week. On Monday he would take back a suitcase of clean clothes which Judy had prepared during the preceding week. Back at Abbotsferry Cottage, he would creep quietly to bed, so as not to disturb Judy. On other occasions, she got up and they talked until dawn about the political events of the week.

Fridays and Saturdays were days for constituency business. This included holding clinics in every part of his constituency so that people could come to discuss their problems with their new Member of Parliament. He also opened bazaars, attended dinners, addressed meetings and performed a hundred and one other duties expected of an MP. On Sundays – but not every Sunday – the Steels attended the nearby Caddonfoot Church to worship. Unlike many people, Steel has not completely rebelled against his strict Sabbatarian upbringing. As a boy he would attend morning and evening service, and Sunday school and Bible class as well.

By Monday morning, the Steels' all too brief weekend together was over, and it was back to London again ...

The cost of this routine battered Steel's family finances. After deducting £230 pension contribution and national insurance, £850 secretary's salary, £800 London living expenses, £40 for telephone bills, £400 car expenses, and £50 for postage and other sundries, Steel calculated he had less than £1,000 a year left from his £3,250 parliamentary salary. And that was before tax. With no savings, no private income, and no family money to call on, Steel had no alternative but to supplement this slender income with earnings from part-time work. Although he had never been trained as a journalist, he built up a considerable practice as a freelance writer during the 1960s and early '70s, which substantially enhanced his income. He also exercised his growing skill as a broadcaster, fronting a series of programmes – mostly in the Sunday evening 'God slot' – for various independent television companies. Since he became leader of the Liberal party, this activity has had to be considerably curtailed.

This journalistic work was sufficiently remunerative to enable the Steels to move out of their rented cottage at Boleside and buy their first home in May 1966. They still live there. The house in Ettrick Bridge is a conversion from three two-roomed cottages built in the late seventeenth century for farm workers on the Duke of Buccleuch's estate. The move was partly prompted by the imminent arrival of the Steel's first child, Graeme, who was born in August.

While highly necessary from a financial point of view, journalistic and broadcasting work was, to some extent, an irritant to Steel. After the euphoria of his stunning election win in March 1965 had worn off, he realised that he might have little more than a year in Parliament before the next election. During the by-election campaign, Steel had massive help from the Liberal party nationally – six professional agents, thousands of volunteer workers, and hundreds of pounds in campaign donations. There was no prospect of this bounty in the next election. He had to rely almost entirely on his own resources.

So, soon after the by-election, the Steels threw themselves into a frenetic round of activity designed to build up the Liberals' slender organisation in Roxburgh, Selkirk and Peebles. A full-time professional agent was appointed, and Steel raced round the constituency to prove he was going to be every bit as good an MP as he had promised. He diligently took up hundreds of grievances on behalf of his constituents, and attended scores of local functions.

The depopulation issue, which he had spotlighted during his election campaign, remained a key political topic in the Borders. Early in 1966, the government published a White Paper on the Borders, based on a special study carried out by the Scottish Economic Planning Council. The White Paper recommended government action to reverse the depopulation trend in the Borders by building new housing and introducing new industry. Steel welcomed this report as it showed he had already been effective in drawing national attention to the problems of the Borders. But he castigated the government for proceeding too slowly. 'The Borders have waited long enough for signs of government action. The inclusion of the Borders development area for 40 per cent investment grants and the intention to appoint a planning consultant and consultative group are steps in the right direction, but the whole process has been painfully slow.'

When the election finally came in March 1966, Steel had firmly established his reputation in the constituency as an active man of the people who could get things done. Nevertheless, he faced tough opposition from new Tory and Labour candidates. After their by-election debacle, the Tories dumped Robin McEwen and chose Ian McIntyre, the 34-year-old head of Information and Research at Scottish Conservative Central Office at Edinburgh, and a former press officer to Sir Alec Douglas Home. Labour chose Colin Lindsay, a young Edinburgh university graduate who lived in Galashiels.

McIntyre, who had played a key role in the Tories' by-election campaign, proved a cunning campaigner. Steel fought the election on his brief record as MP. He spent most of the campaign in his constituency, making only five TV broadcasts during the campaign. He shared a Liberal party political broadcast with Jeremy Thorpe. After Thorpe had launched a characteristically ebullient attack on the British military presence east of Suez, accompanied by the strains of 'Colonel Bogey', Steel gave a more sober appraisal of British industrial relations. Critics praised the broadcast for its effectiveness.

The pundits predicted Steel would hold his seat. On polling day he found his majority reduced to 2,211, mostly caused by some of Steel's realigned voters swinging back to Labour. Tory women screamed hysterically 'Go home, Steel' as he tried to make his victory speech from the steps of Jedburgh Town Hall. But he had reason to be well pleased. A study of Liberal by-election wins shows that those MPs who hold their seats at the first general election after the by-election can usually expect a long parliamentary career.

6

End of the Grimond era

When Jo Grimond addressed his first Liberal assembly as party leader in the autumn of 1957, he told the cheering delegates, 'In the next ten years, it is a question of get on or get out. Let us make it get on.' By 1965, he had decided it was time to get out. During December of that year, he discussed with his closest confidants, veteran Liberal peer Lord Byers, brother-in-law Mark Bonham Carter and MP Jeremy Thorpe, his desire to stand down. They persuaded him to stay on until at least the next general election, which could be only months away. Steel had not been privy to these discussions, and he only found out about them when Grimond issued a press statement early in January 1966 confirming that he intended to stay on as leader, thus firmly quashing any rumours that he might be planning an early departure.

For some time, Grimond had been tiring of the gruelling routine of being Liberal leader, trailing round the same town halls making the same speeches year after year, forever forecasting the dawn of a Liberal revival which never quite came. But he had also been deeply disappointed by the way in which the party had reacted to his suggestion that Liberals should be prepared to co-operate with the Labour government, if it lost its overall parliamentary majority. This marked a decided failure in Grimond's political career, and also an important point in Steel's political development.

For years, Grimond had been making speeches at Liberal conferences about the need for a radical realignment. The delegates, workers from the constituencies, had roundly cheered him, for Grimond was a fine platform orator in his prime who communicated an infectious enthusiasm to his audiences. Yet those same delegates who cheered Grimond's speeches reacted like frightened maidens as soon as a real prospect of parliamentary realignment presented itself.

65

When Grimond floated the idea of working with Harold Wilson's Labour government on an agreed programme of radical but non-socialist measures, hundreds of constituency workers, and several MPs, ran for cover. Steel was not among them. As we have seen, along with Jeremy Thorpe, he was one of only two Liberal MPs, apart from Grimond, who supported the idea of a parliamentary arrangement with Labour. He actively and enthusiastically argued the case for Grimond's proposal, but with little effect. He agreed with Grimond's colourful comment at the 1965 Liberal assembly that Liberals now had 'their teeth in the real red meat of politics'. But this red meat proved too much of a meal for the rest of the party to stomach. As it became increasingly clear that he could not carry his party with him, Grimond gradually dropped the idea during the autumn and winter of 1965.

Steel is a great learner of political lessons. And he learnt an important lesson from this small but significant episode in recent Liberal party history, the lesson being that a party leader is only in a position to seize a political opportunity if he receives general backing from the rest of his party. It follows from this that, if a party leader is to be certain of backing for a particular policy, he must test the water before that opportunity presents itself. Although Grimond had talked in an abstract kind of way about radical realignment, he had not educated his party in the practical implications of how this would affect the way the party would operate in Parliament. Thus, the notion that the Liberals should co-operate with Labour came as an unexpected and unwelcome idea to many Liberal activists. Steel describes Grimond as 'cautious, easy-going and vague', and it is this vagueness which was Grimond's undoing. Not enough party members truly understood the political and parliamentary consequences of Grimond's philosophical talk about radical realignment.

In the spring of 1966, Wilson called a general election, which he won with a comfortable majority of nearly one hundred seats. The Liberals increased their parliamentary representation by two, but their influence on the government was now negligible. The Liberal teeth were no longer in the red meat of politics – and, in any event, as Steel had pointed out those teeth had proved to be false. Grimond soldiered on unenthusiastically for a few more months after the election, but decided the time had now definitely come to quit. This time he kept his decision entirely to himself for fear that someone like the highly persuasive Jeremy Thorpe would talk him out of it again.

Apart from Grimond's wife, Laura, Steel was the first to learn of Grimond's intention to stand down as party leader. In January 1967, Steel, his wife and baby son, Graeme, went to spend a weekend with the Grimonds at their home, The Old Manse, in Kirkwall, in the Orkney Islands. Steel had been there once before, as a student, but it was Judy's first visit. The visit had been planned as part politics and part holiday. Steel was to address a couple of meetings in support of Grimond, and then spend the rest of the weekend relaxing, away from the pressures of his own constituency. But this plan was scuppered on the first evening of Steel's stay.

Before Steel set off for an evening engagement to speak, Grimond calmly summoned him into his study. He told him that the following week he intended to resign as Liberal party leader. He was going to tell his constituency officers over the weekend, and the parliamentary Liberal party at the beginning of the following week. Steel recalls the meeting: 'I was quite shattered. It was fairly devastating, especially as I had been a disciple of Grimond Liberalism, and this was my first visit as an MP to his constituency.' Steel did not try to persuade Grimond to change his mind. He says, 'I think I indicated that I was horrified, but he had by that time made up his mind, and he was telling me, not consulting me.'

Grimond had, in fact, told Steel this devastating news before the meeting to prevent the embarrassment of Steel launching into a paeon of praise about Grimond's leadership of the Liberal party. At the meeting, Steel stumbled through his speech, his mind quite clearly on other things.

During the weekend, Grimond and Steel discussed the future leadership of the party. Grimond had no doubts about who his heir apparent was. He backed Jeremy Thorpe, and Steel supported this. During his brief period in Parliament, Steel had become a warm admirer of Thorpe. He liked his irreverence, his drive and iconoclasm. Like Thorpe, Steel was on the left wing of the party, taking a strong stand on racialism, Rhodesia, and human rights, and backing measures to increase public spending in order to relieve poverty. Thorpe had turned up to campaign for several days in Steel's victorious fight for the Roxburgh by-election, unlike many of the other MPs, who made only fleeting visits. Although Thorpe was, on the surface, a showman, an extrovert and a bit of a clown, Steel recognised that underneath the buffoonery was a committed radical, like himself. During their discussion, both Grimond and Steel agreed that Thorpe was the natural choice as leader because he had the necessary drive to do the job. 'It didn't seem that anyone else was a natural contender, although we didn't know at that stage who would actually stand,' recalls Steel.

After the weekend, Grimond flew south to London to break the news to the party and to fellow MPs. By the time Steel arrived in London on Tuesday morning – he had stayed in Scotland on Monday to complete some engagements – rumours were already flying thick and fast, and the campaigning had begun. The official announcement about Grimond's retirement was made on Tuesday afternoon, and immediately hit the headlines in the evening papers. The announcement also stated that the election of a new leader would take place at one o'clock the following afternoon, Wednesday, leaving only twenty-four hours between the resignation and the election.

This announcement created immediate fury amongst ordinary party members. The heads of the party organisation had been given the distinct impression the day before that the election would not take place until Thursday, leaving time for consultation between the party's MPs and the membership in the country. On hearing the news that the election would take place the next day, party members felt that they had been stabbed in the back, and they started to bombard the MPs with telegrams and phone calls demanding that the election should be postponed.

While rage among the party members built up, the parliamentary Liberal party embarked upon a vicious little power struggle in which Steel played a critical role. Political pundits and newspaper columnists were amazed at the ferocity of the leadership fight. Veteran *Evening Standard* political columnist Robert Carvel commented, 'Having observed at close quarters Labour and Tory in-fighting in recent years, I give the Liberals First Division status right now.'

What astonished political observers was how a small political party of only a dozen beleaguered Members could fall out amongst themselves quite so comprehensively. To begin with, three of the twelve Members were nominated as candidates in the election. In addition to Thorpe, there was Eric Lubbock, the party's chief whip and MP for Orpington, and Emlyn Hooson, reckoned to be on the right of the party, a brilliant Welsh QC and the MP for Montgomeryshire. These three candidates competed for votes amongst the other nine MPs. The whole contest had a faintly ridiculous air, like children fighting to be king of the castle. Despite this, as Tuesday evening wore on, mini campaigns developed amongst the MPs. Suddenly Grimond's complacent assumption that Thorpe would succeed him as the natural heir apparent, seemed far from certain.

Had the party elected its leader by the first-past-the-post electoral system used in Westminster elections, the likely outcome would have been clearer. In fact, the election took place by the system of the single transferable vote, appropriately for a party which consistently argued for proportional representation. Under the single transferable vote system, if the top candidate in the first ballot does not obtain an overall majority of votes cast, the bottom candidate drops out and his votes are redistributed amongst the other candidates. This meant that if Thorpe failed to get seven votes on the first ballot, the voters' second choices would be critically important.

That Tuesday evening, Steel took charge as Thorpe's unofficial campaign manager and performed some alarming sums on the back of an envelope. This revealed that Thorpe had only four definite first-choice votes: himself, Steel, Grimond and John Pardoe, the young MP for North Cornwall. Lubbock had support from north-country MPs Michael Winstanley and Richard Wainwright. Hooson received backing from Scots MPs Alastair McKenzie (Ross and Cromarty) and Russell Johnston (Inverness). This left two MPs unaccounted for – Peter Bessell and James Davidson.

Bessell, a free-wheeling businessman, had won Bodmin at the 1964 general election. In his years in politics, he had built up quite a reputation in the West Country, second only to that of Thorpe. Both he and Thorpe were close allies, and Thorpe had frequently helped Bessell in his political campaigns. Steel canvassed Bessell and was assured that he would be voting for Thorpe. But later that evening Steel discovered, by talking to other Liberal MPs, that Bessell had also pledged his support to Hooson. For the normally sedate Liberal party, this was skulduggery of a high order. Bessell's ambivalence meant that Steel could not definitely pencil him into the Thorpe column, which left Thorpe with still only four votes, the other candidates each with three, and the potential to score five, if they could mop up both the floaters.

Throughout Tuesday night, the battle for these two votes continued at Westminster. With Bessell still uncertain, Steel went in search of James Davidson, the newly elected MP for West Aberdeenshire. Davidson, who had won his seat at the previous election, was a former diplomat, had the looks of a Hollywood matinée idol, and was regarded as Westminster's incorruptible Mr Clean. Steel knew he would get a straight answer from him.

He finally tracked Davidson down in the tiny office the two shared with three other Liberal MPs in the St Stephen's Tower, above the public entrance to the House of Commons. Steel and Davidson got on well and had a mutual respect for each other. It was already gone midnight when they started to discuss the future leadership of the party. Davidson frankly told Steel that he was inclined to vote for Eric Lubbock, but doubted whether he had the charisma for the job. Davidson expressed doubts about Thorpe's policy stand on some issues. As a former diplomat, he felt uneasy about Thorpe's demand at the previous Liberal assembly that a Rhodesian railway line should be bombed in order to stop supplies getting through to the illegal Smith regime. Steel suggested that Davidson should receive reassurance from Thorpe himself on these issues. Although it was past midnight, he rang Thorpe at his flat, and the two trooped round there for an early morning meeting. It was nearly 2.00 a.m. when they arrived. Despite the early hour, Thorpe switched on the charm, and Davidson left having committed his vote.

When Steel reached his office shortly after breakfast time, he found a groundswell of opinion building up inside the party against holding the election so soon. The parliamentary party had fixed a meeting for later that morning to discuss proposals to delay the election. However, Steel sent his apologies. He was scheduled to spend the morning in committee with Dr Michael Winstanley discussing his Abortion Bill, which was now at a crucial stage. But Steel let his colleagues know that he wanted the election to go ahead on schedule. He was concerned about a 'Stop Jeremy' movement which was said to be building up in the constituencies, especially in the north of England.

In the election at one o'clock, Thorpe received six votes (including, in the end Bessell's), and Lubbock and Hooson three each. Lubbock and Hooson retired gracefully, and Thorpe was elected unanimously on the second ballot held immediately after. Steel had played an important role in seeing his candidate safely home to victory. He had, of course, cast his first-preference vote for Thorpe. His second choice went to Lubbock.

Steel was well rewarded by Thorpe for his staunch support during the leadership campaign. In a reshuffle of parliamentary jobs which followed Thorpe's election, Steel became spokesman on Commonwealth affairs, the job Thorpe had previously held and an important post in view of the continuing Rhodesia crisis. It was the parliamentary portfolio he most wanted. A year later, Steel also took on the job of Scottish whip, when Russell Johnston stood down to concentrate on other work. The practical effect of this was to provide Steel with a better and more central office, which he shared with Eric Lubbock.

The haste with which the election took place had future implications for the party. The groundswell of opinion from party members meant that the whole question of how the leader was to be elected in the future would be a matter for intense debate.

Under Thorpe, the Liberal party mounted a grandiose campaign with the title The Great Crusade. It was launched at a rally in the Albert Hall, the highspot of which was the appearance of Thorpe. With characteristic showmanship, he leapt into a spotlight to a fanfare flourish, amidst wild cheering from supporters. However, the campaign never got off the ground, and failed to achieve its objectives of boosting party membership and raising more funds. Steel played only a small part in the campaign. He had never taken much interest in the details of party organisation outside Scotland and his own constituency.

During the remainder of the 1960s, Steel became involved with a number of cross-party campaigns on a wide range of subjects.

Dissatisfaction with the Thorpe leadership grew swiftly over the next few years, especially among the Young Liberals and more left-wing sections of the party. It culminated in an attempted *putsch* while Thorpe was on his honeymoon. Thorpe returned

71

from honeymoon and demanded a vote of confidence from the party's National Executive Committee, which he won with an overwhelming majority. Steel knew nothing about the plot against Thorpe, even though he was closer to the Young Liberals than most MPs. He was, however, regarded as a Thorpe supporter and thus was not party to the plans to dethrone the leader.

Although Steel remained loyal to Thorpe during this period, he had considerable reservations about the way in which Thorpe was leading the party, and especially about the lack of a coherent political strategy to capture support from radical voters disillusioned by the conservatism and failures of Harold Wilson's government. Steel believed that Thorpe's undoubted enthusiasm and energy would have been more productive had it been directed to achieving more clearly defined political objectives.

But for the time being, Steel was distracted from the mainstream of Liberal party affairs by his own parliamentary attempt to reform the law on abortion.

7

The young legislator

At the beginning of each new parliamentary session, a curious raffle takes place in a House of Commons committee room. The room is normally filled with MPs anxiously awaiting the result of the draw, and the chairman of the Ways and Means Committee pulls the tickets out of the hat. But this is no draw for a Christmas hamper or a horse in a Derby sweepstake. It is an important part of Britain's legislative process. The draw decides the order of precedence which MPs will have during the coming session in introducing Private Member's Bills.

In practice, although some four hundred Members habitually enter the draw, only those who draw the top half-dozen places stand anything like a chance of seeing their chosen bill become law, such is the pressure on parliamentary time. Despite this, vital subjects, such as the reform of the law relating to divorce, homosexuality and capital punishment – subjects calculated to stir the passions of the British people – have been dealt with by private Member's legislation. Some people find it more than odd that reform on matters like these should depend literally on the luck of the draw. Others merely shrug their shoulders and point to the declining importance of private Member's legislation in Britain's Parliament.

Another curious feature of the whole process is that most Members who enter the draw have no idea what bill they will introduce if they succeed in winning a top place. So when the chairman of the Ways and Means Committee drew David Steel's name out of the hat for the third place in the private Members' ballot at the beginning of the 1966–7 parliamentary session, Steel had no inkling that by the end of that same session he would have piloted through the Commons an item of legislation that was described as one of the most significant pieces of social reform of the twentieth century. This event turned him, a new MP of less than two years' standing, into a national figure as well known as many cabinet ministers and MPs who had been in the House for twenty years of more. It was, perhaps, another remarkable example of Steel's facility to be in the right place at the right time. But there is no doubt that in piloting his controversial Abortion Act on to the statute book, Steel made his parliamentary and national reputation.

The MPs who enter the committee room where the draw is made may not have an idea for a bill when they go in, but when they come out there are plenty of people who will help them find a worthy subject. Representatives of scores of pressure groups, covering subjects ranging from blood sports to Sunday observance, hover outside the committee room on the day of the draw, waiting to bend the ear of any lucky MP to their pet cause. So within an hour of the draw taking place, Steel was sitting on one of the green benches in the dimly lit central lobby discussing abortion law reform with Vera Houghton and Alastair Service of the Abortion Law Reform Association (ALRA). They had just come from a meeting with Edwin Brooks, the Labour MP for Bebington, who had drawn seventh place in the ballot. He had made a firm offer to introduce an abortion reform bill, but his seventh place gave him only a slender chance of being successful.

Steel listened sympathetically to the earnest case put by Houghton and Service, who told him of the suffering that Britain's harsh abortion laws, unreformed since Victorian times, inflicted on women. At the previous general election, he had promised, in response to lobbying, to vote for abortion law reform, but he was non-committal; when he emerged from the committee room an hour earlier, Liberal peer the Earl of Arran had button-holed Steel to seek support in his attempt to reform the law on homosexuality.

Arran, who had only recently joined the Liberals from the cross-benches of the Lords because, he said, he could hear debates better from the Liberal seats, made out a compelling case. He pointed out that the Liberal party Council had recently called for homosexual law reform, and that the issue deeply affected personal liberty. He said that as many as a million people could be affected by this law, whereas fewer would be affected by abortion law reform. He asserted that Steel would get more support in the Commons for homosexual rather than abortion law reform. Again, Steel listened sympathetically, but kept his counsel.

During the next few days, dozens of organisations pressed Steel to favour their causes. At various times he was invited to abolish fox-hunting, push for noise abatement, help small shopkeepers, introduce proportional representation, reform divorce, stop vivisection, ban immigration, and make Scotland independent. He also had his own pet subject. At his highly publicised by-election, and at the subsequent general election, he had vigorously called for a Border development authority to be set up by the government. Should he now introduce a bill to set up such an authority? During the next eleven days, he agonised over his decision.

The way in which he reached that decision tells a great deal about the kind of politician Steel is. In doing things like introducing an Abortion Act, opposing a rugby tour in his sports-loving constituency, or taking the Liberal party into a pact with an unpopular Labour government, Steel is often portrayed as a politician who takes unacceptable risks. In fact, this is not so. He is certainly a politician who is prepared to take a stand on principle. Certain subjects, he believes, are worth standing up for, and, if necessary, being defeated for at the next election. For example, Steel would never compromise on anything that was racialist.

On the other hand, Steel very carefully assesses the political risks of any course of action before taking a decision. He is also an expert at minimising the risks of an electorally unpopular course of action. He does this largely by the way in which he argues his case, constantly seeking such common ground as there may be with his opponents by deploying his case in a conciliatory way, rather than by forcefully confronting his opposition. In effect, Steel presents a highly controversial case as uncontroversially as possible. He learnt early on that in a marginal constituency there is a limit to the number of people you can afford to offend.

The other feature of Steel's political character which guided him was his intensely practical approach to politics. Steel is in politics to get things done, and he judges the effectiveness of himself, as well as of others, by what is actually achieved at the end of the day. In this case, he knew that his pipe-dream of a Border development authority stood little chance of reaching the statute book as a private Member's measure. It was far too specialised a subject and would not attract the sustained voting support from other MPs needed to carry a Private Member's Bill.

Moreover, Scottish Secretary William Ross warned Steel publicly and privately that he would oppose such a bill vehemently. This certainly meant that Labour Members would be whipped into the lobby against it, so that it would fall at the first hurdle – the second-reading debate.

After sifting through the dozens of suggestions which reached him, Steel concluded there were really only two practical and worthwhile alternatives – abortion and homosexual law reform. He asked the Home Secretary, Roy Jenkins, to brief him on the current state of the law on both these subjects. Jenkins and his Home Office team hoped Steel would opt for homosexual law reform. Steel went to the Home Office and had a long discussion with Viscount Stoneham and Dick Taverne, both under-secretaries of state. Both tried to persuade him to promote a Sexual Offences Bill, but Steel remained non-committal.

He knew that whichever subject he chose would provoke a storm of protest and controversy, including controversy amongst his constituents. He also had an eye on his slender 2,211 majority, and he did not want his Private Member's Bill to result in his unseating at the next election. Through letters published in newspapers in his constituency, Steel invited his constituents to give him their suggestions on the nature of his private legislation. However, Steel left them in no doubt about the kind of measure he planned to promote. 'I am not willing to use this opportunity as a propaganda exercise. I am not willing to introduce a bill to give effect to some praiseworthy item of Liberal policy which is opposed by the other parties and which would therefore cause the bill to be defeated at the first hurdle. This would result in a waste of the rare opportunity for a private Member to secure some item of legislation, however large or small.' Apart from this, Steel sounded the party managers in his constituency. They told him bluntly that homosexual reform was unacceptable, but they were not so violently opposed to abortion law reform. In any case, Scottish law already took a somewhat more liberal view of abortion than English law. So eleven days after being approached by Houghton and Service of ALRA, Steel delighted them by announcing that he would promote an abortion reform bill.

We must pause here to consider the daunting position in which Steel now found himself. At the age of twenty-eight, and with barely eighteen months' parliamentary experience behind him, he planned to pilot, almost single-handed, a controversial measure through Parliament. Moreover, he planned to do this without the resources of a government minister, which would normally include a battalion of highly briefed civil servants to feed him with research and speech material. Steel started from the position that he knew next to nothing about abortion and the case for abortion law reform, and very little about the parliamentary tactics of piloting a bill through the Commons. In fact, Steel looked barely old enough to marry, let alone be a Member of Parliament, and certainly not old enough to be planning to legislate for the moral minefield of abortion. Set against these disadvantages, Steel did have a sound legal training and a super-cool temperament, which helped him keep his head when many of the more excitable supporters and opponents started to trade vicious insults. Steel also brought to the task a capacity for incredibly hard work, and a tough independent judgement, which at times exasperated his supporters as well as his opponents.

Two people who watched him closely throughout the year-long fight for the Abortion Bill were Madeleine Simms and Keith Hindell of the ALRA. In their book *Abortion Law Reformed* (Peter Owen, London, 1971) they summed up Steel's contribution. 'Abortion was his first bill, but he continually demonstrated his mastery of the brief both in making his own prepared speeches and in countering points made by his opponents. Throughout months of discussion he kept his good temper in the face of the most aggravating filibuster. Outside the Chamber, ALRA found him businesslike if inexperienced in dealing with some other MPs and with the grand eminences of the medical profession.'

Steel's Medical Termination of Pregnancy Bill, as it was originally called, was published on 15 June 1966. It was by no means the first attempt to reform the law on abortion. Since 1953 there had been half a dozen or more unsuccessful attempts to change the law. The law still dated from the draconian Offences Against the Persons Act of 1861. This threatened any woman who tried to get an abortion with penal servitude for life or with imprisonment for up to two years, with hard labour and solitary confinement thrown in for good measure. Although case law had amended this during the intervening century, it was still far from easy to obtain a legal abortion, and expert opinion reckoned that dozens of women died every year as the result of inexpertly conducted illegal abortions.

The Bill which Steel introduced was largely based on a measure piloted through the House of Lords the previous session by septuagenarian peer Lord Silkin. It had not, of course, become law, because it had not passed the Commons.

The Bill set out four main grounds for abortion. These were:

− that continued pregnancy would involve serious risk to the life or physical or mental health of the mother-to-be at or after the child's birth;

− that there was a substantial risk that the child would be born suffering from physical or mental abnormalities which would prove a serious handicap;

− that the pregnant woman's capacity as a mother would be severely overstrained by the care of a child or another child;

− that the pregnant woman was a defective or became pregnant while under the age of sixteen or because of rape.

These proposals had been drawn up by a committee consisting of the Bill's twelve parliamentary sponsors, five representatives of ALRA and Lord Silkin. Steel's parliamentary backers included Dr Michael Winstanley, the doctor-MP for Cheadle, Dame Joan Vickers, the doughty Tory lady from Plymouth, Devonport, Mrs Renee Short, the fiery Socialist MP for Wolverhampton North East, and Lord Lambton, the Conservative MP for Berwick, who later resigned from Parliament following a call-girl scandal.

Steel introduced the Bill in a speech at the start of the second-reading debate on 22 July 1966 − the most important speech of his parliamentary career so far. The speech was quiet, reasoned, unemotional and workmanlike. Beside him on the bench, the second up below the gangway, stood a foot-high pile of correspondence he had already received on the issue. Steel started by explaining why he had not introduced a measure to promote his favoured Border development authority. 'There is an issue of principle involved,' he told a hushed chamber, 'in that the opportunity to introduce a Private Member's Bill is an almost unique one, which in my opinion should not be used to express a particular point of view for party advantage, perhaps with an eye to the next election. I think it should be used for something positive − whether it be a major or minor reform − which can have a reasonable prospect of arriving on the statute book.' This was the point that Steel had already made forcefully to his constituents.

He then described how he had approached the drafting of the Bill. 'The difficulty in drafting a bill of this kind is to decide how and where to draw the line. We want to stamp out the back-street abortions, but it is not the intention of the promoters of the Bill to leave a wide-open door for abortion on request.'

Steel continued, 'If the Bill becomes law, it will become possible for a patient to consult her family doctor freely and openly about her pregnancy and about the possible termination of the pregnancy. At present, the whole question is surrounded by so much whispering and so much doubt about the legality that the effect is that the last person, very often, with whom a woman wishes to discuss it is her family doctor.

'It may well be that in many cases the effect of introducing the Bill will be that, instead of a woman having a back-street abortion, she will discuss the matter with her family doctor, in some way be reassured and feel that she has been offered some guidance and no abortion will take place at all.' Steel then set out his approach to the tricky task of steering the Bill through the Commons. He said he would be prepared to accept amendments to his Bill, except from those who opposed it on principle. This was the conciliatory Steel at work, building the widest possible support for a controversial measure. Steel then bluntly challenged Catholic MPs, like Norman St John Stevas, to take note of an opinion poll which revealed that more than 50 per cent of the Catholics questioned wanted abortion law changed.

He ended his speech, 'The report of the Social and Moral Welfare Board of the Church of Scotland quotes a German theologian as stating that human life in every form is sacrosanct but that we have to ask ourselves what quantitive item of sacrosanctity may be attached to each form of life – the ovum fertilised, the moving embryo, the born child and the mother. He said, "A paper-thin wall separates us from sacrilege – all such decisions can be made only under saving grace – such dangers always go with freedom. Those who want to avoid the dangers only do so by setting up a rigid dogma ... So there is obviously no perfect solution. The decision has to be taken in the light of God's understanding of our human frailty." '

The debate showed Steel's ability to master a complex subject and present a compelling case, although his speech lacked histrionics and the kind of quotable quotes which newspaper headline-writers love.

After Steel's speech, opponent William Wells, the Labour MP for Wallsall North, pointedly challenged Steel to say what his feelings would be if his daughter became a nurse and had to perform abortions. 'What does he think his feelings will be if his daughter becomes a nurse and if, when he sees her at the weekend, and says, "What have you been doing darling?" she answers, "I have been in the operating theatre terminating pregnancies and I have burned six embryos." ' Steel's supporters howled their rage at Wells. But the principal of the attack remained icy cool. Despite a spirited counterattack by the Bill's opponents, it sailed through its second reading by 223 votes to 29, a larger majority than its supporters had expected.

Steel now entered upon one of the most difficult periods of his political career. The small vote against his Bill at the second reading had understated the extent of opposition to it. During the summer recess, which lasted into November, and immediately after Parliament reassembled, opposition to the Bill mounted. In order to become law, the Bill had to pass through a committee stage, where it would be considered in detail line by line, then a report stage in the full Commons, where changes to it could be debated again, and finally through a third-reading debate. And then it would have to pass through the same process in the House of Lords. This was a parliamentary minefield, and at an early stage Steel recognised that his Bill would need several important changes if it were to stand a chance of completing its remaining stages successfully.

In a sense, Steel was like a general fighting a battle on a number of different fronts simultaneously. He had to deal with the professional medical associations, which objected to parts of the Bill, the Churches, which also objected to parts of it, and sundry other opponents in Parliament, the country and his constituency. Then he also had to deal with his supporters, in and outside Parliament, ALRA, and militant feminist organisations. Many of these wanted his Bill to go further than he planned. Steel's task was to steer a path between the welter of conflicting advice he received, so that the Bill could command a sufficient parliamentary majority.

At times, he upset everyone, including ALRA, in performing this difficult task, but in the end few of his supporters could argue that his judgement had erred. The Bill passed through its remaining stages with much narrower parliamentary majorities, and only by grace of the government's providing extra time for its debate.

In the aftermath of the passing of the Act, Steel was criticised by supporters for conceding too much to opponents, and by opponents for not conceding enough. It is difficult to see, however, that a more wide-ranging abortion act would have passed through Parliament, whilst a more restrictive act would not have made a large enough change in the law to meet the objectives Steel had in mind.

As Steel saw it, the key to passing the Bill was to retain the support of a body of middle opinion in the Commons, who did not have strong feelings about the law on abortion, and who would be frightened off if they felt they were being asked to support too radical a measure. These members – like all MPs – came under increased pressure from the Bill's opponents after the second-reading debate. The large majority in favour of the Bill alerted opponents to the possibility of its passing through Parliament, and they marshalled their forces against it.

Many MPs become nervous about supporting measures of social reform, such as abortion, when placed under pressure by angry constituents. And Churches and pressure groups organised letter-writing and lobbying campaigns to make their views known to MPs. Steel received more letters than anyone – thousands during the passage of the Bill. Many of them were anonymous and abusive, comparing him to a cross between Herod and Hitler. In the end, he only answered those from his constituents or which had an original point to make. He passed the most abusive letters to Labour MP and former sociology lecturer Peter Jackson, who made a study of them.

Steel realised that if the moderate, middle-of-the-road MPs were not to be frightened off supporting his Bill, he would have to show that it received support from a body of informed opinion. This meant convincing the medical profession that the measure was needed and worth while. However, the medical associations, which act as spokesmen for the medical profession, are inherently conservative, and Steel never persuaded them to give enthusiastic endorsement to his measure, except for the Royal Medico-Psychological Association. The Royal College of Gynaecologists had stated, 'The majority of gynaecologists in this country can see no urgent need to reform the law on abortion.' But they conceded that some reform of abortion law was inevitable, and urged that abortions should only be carried out where there was a 'substantial risk that the child if born would suffer from such physical or mental abnormalities as to deprive it of any prospect of reasonable enjoyment of life'. The British Medical Association also produced a report. It argued that the conditions for an abortion should not be too closely defined by the law, in case patients put too much pressure on doctors for abortions in specific circumstances. The BMA opposed some of the wide-ranging conditions for abortion set out in Steel's original bill.

In a series of negotiations, which stretched through November and December, Steel tried to win wider support for his Bill from the medical profession. He had, of course, his medical supporters. Mr Peter Diggory, a noted consultant gynaecologist, was a close adviser of Steel throughout the passage of the Bill.

In November, Steel travelled to Aberdeen to meet two eminent medical supporters of abortion reform: Sir Dugald Baird, professor of gynaecology at the University of Aberdeen, and Dr Malcolm Millar, professor of mental health. Over a long lunch, Steel discussed the problems that bothered him about the subject. The meeting marked a watershed in his handling of the Bill. He emerged from this meeting with a deeper insight into the issues surrounding the subject, and from then on dealt with supporters and opponents more confidently.

Despite this, Steel reduced the scope of his Bill after pressure from the BMA and RCOG. Just before flying back to Ettrick Bridge to spend the Christmas of 1966 with his family, Steel announced that he planned to withdraw the clauses in his Bill which allowed for a woman to have an abortion if another child would overstrain her capacities as a mother or if she had been raped. Steel's new amendment, which would be debated in the committee session of the Bill, provided for a woman to have an abortion if her physical or mental well-being was at risk. In determining this, her doctor could take into account, 'the patient's total environment actual or reasonably forseeable'.

Steel acknowledged that the BMA, the RCOG and the Church

of England had played a part in helping to frame this new amendment. But it outraged his supporters in ALRA, who felt the new grounds for abortion were far too restrictive. After the Bill had been passed, ALRA acknowledged that Steel had been right to reduce the scope of the Bill in view of the difficulty it had passing through its remaining parliamentary stages.

Back in Ettrick Bridge, Steel realised that he had some constituency fences to mend. Many of the 3,000 Catholics in his constituency were outraged by his Bill. Steel played the conciliator. He went to address an audience of local student priests. He told them that though he disagreed with their opinions he deeply respected them. He hoped they would respect his opinions even though they disagreed with them. They politely applauded.

More disappointing, Steel noted that the Church of Scotland had come out against his Bill. This was especially upsetting as his father was a minister in the Church. When Steel first proposed his Bill, the Church had not pronounced on the issue. With a liberal attitude to abortion in Scotland, Steel hoped the Church would give his Bill at least grudging approval. The Church of Scotland wanted abortion reform, but only where the mother's health or well-being were threatened. It bluntly stated that Steel's Bill went too far. Despite this, many individual ministers of the Church supported him, including some in his own constituency. Others truculently opposed him. Minister George Duncan, of St George's Tron Church, Glasgow, banned him from presenting a religious television programme from the church, because he disagreed with Steel's views on abortion. 'I felt it would be wrong to have him on a programme going out from our church to the rest of the nation,' he uncharitably complained.

Back at Westminster, the committee stage of the Bill started in early January. Every Wednesday morning for twelve weeks, Steel and the other twenty-nine members of the committee assembled in committee room 10 for a bout of verbal fencing. From the start, it was clear that the opponents of the Bill intended to fight it to the finish. Steel's backers had an in-built majority on the committee. But the opponents, such as Labour MP Simon Mahon, and Tories Jill Knight and Bernard Braine, had another weapon – the filibuster. For hours on end they talked at length round each amendment. During these verbose interludes, Steel relaxed back on the benches, waiting for them to run out of words.

The Bill emerged from the committee much as Steel had wanted it. But it now faced the most critical phase of its parliamentary passage, the report stage and third reading. Because the Bill had been substantially changed in committee, all the changes could be debated again at the report stage of the Bill. And the government had allotted only one day's sitting for the report stage and third reading. If it failed to complete its passage in this time, it would automatically drop to the bottom of the queue for Private Member's Bills, and stand little chance of passing into law by the end of the parliamentary session.

Before this day's debate took place, it was clear that the Bill could not possibly pass in the time available. Steel, supported by Labour MPs Douglas Houghton and Charles Pannell, talked to the Home Secretary, Roy Jenkins, government chief whip Jon Silkin, and leader of the House, Richard Crossman. They agreed to provide time for an all-night sitting so that the Bill could be completed. This acrimonious all-night sitting took place on 29 June, but after twelve hours of talk the amendments to clause one of the Bill had still not been completed.

Steel desperately needed more time. Again he went to see Crossman in his room at the House. Over drinks, Crossman gave Steel a brisk headmasterly lecture on the errors in his tactics. He pointed out that the parliamentary timetable was already crowded, and that, although he personally had sympathy for Steel's Bill, the government could not be seen to be favouring a private Member's measure. Steel told Crossman that unless the issue was decided one way or another, it would crop up year after year, encroaching on valuable parliamentary time. Crossman and Jenkins once again appealed to the cabinet for more time, and in the event a final sitting was arranged after normal parliamentary business on 13 July. It was a debate to the finish – the House would sit until it had completed all stages of the Bill one way or the other. The opponents knew now that they must be defeated, and after another all-night sitting, Steel finally moved the third reading of the Bill at 9.45 on the morning of the 14 July.

Even then, the saga of the Abortion Bill, as it had become known by now, had not finished. By a majority of one, the House of Lords passed a wrecking amendment. Steel threatened to invoke the Parliament Act, which allows a bill to become law despite the opposition of the Lords if it is passed by the Commons in two successive parliamentary sessions. The Lords backed down, and the Bill passed into law on 26 October 1967, when it received the Royal Assent. Ironically, Steel was not present to witness the triumph. He was in a plane over the Atlantic on his way to join a parliamentary delegation at the United Nations.

Far from settling the law on abortion, the passing of Steel's Bill opened up a decade of debate on the subject. In the intervening period, there have been at least four attempts to restrict the gains made in Steel's legislation. None of these has succeeded, although Steel supported a measure in a bill presented by Scottish MP John Corrie to cut the time limit for an abortion from twenty-eight weeks to twenty-four weeks from the date of conception. This move echoed a recommendation of the Lane Committee, which was set up in the early 1970s to study the working of the new abortion law. It concluded that few major changes were needed. The Lane Committee said, 'We have no doubt that the gains facilitated by the Act have much outweighed any disadvantages for which it has been criticised.'

Steel himself modestly describes the Act as a 'relatively minor but significant social reform in our country'. Others have been more fulsome about the measure. Whatever the truth, it undoubtedly made his parliamentary reputation. After the Bill had passed the Commons, twenty-five Members from all parties signed a Commons motion congratulating Steel on 'the parliamentary skill and ability shown by him, and the admirable manner in which he piloted this difficult and contentious bill through its various stages in the House of Commons'.

The more zealous of Steel's opponents have depicted him as an enthusiast for abortion. In fact, he does not like it. He thinks there are too many abortions. He wants to see the wider availability of free contraception to reduce the number of abortions.

He says, 'There is a great deal of loose talk about the permissive society. We are not a less moral society than previous generations, but we do talk more openly about it. I still want to prevent the need for abortion ever arising, and because I proposed the abortion law does not mean I agree with the opinions of other people who supported it. Abortion is, I am afraid, being used as a contraceptive. The present level is too high. I agree with medical

85

opinion that free contraception should be available on the National Health, otherwise people will accept free abortion instead, because they either cannot or will not pay for contraceptives. It worries me greatly.'

Steel adds, 'Abortion has undoubtedly brought a lot of happiness. One does not expect women who have had one to go round saying so, but doctors who deal with these patients tell me it has meant a great deal to them. Free abortion and contraception may have a marginal effect on moral laxity. But it is much more important to avoid unwanted pregnancy, though I agree it is important to prevent any addition to the decline in morals. Abortion on demand need not follow free contraception. The decision to have an abortion is much more fundamental than one to use a contraceptive and must remain in the hands of the doctor. The Act says there must be a real need, and I stick to that.'

Steel learnt more about the intricacies of parliamentary procedure during his year piloting the Abortion Act through Parliament than many members learn in a lifetime in the House. The testing experience also thickened his skin. In the end, he became blasé about the abuse which was hurled at him.

Yet perhaps the really significant developments of the exercise were in Steel's political attitudes. For Steel, brought up on Jo Grimond's talk of radical realignment, here was an example of radicals working together to achieve practical reform. Many of the young Labour Members with whom Steel worked – and the odd left-wing Tory, like Sir George Sinclair, MP for Dorking – were the sort of people Grimond and Steel would have liked to have in a new radical party. If this kind of positive and effective activity could work on abortion reform, why not on other issues, reasoned Steel. Not for the last time in his political career, Steel was to get political satisfaction from working in a cross-party campaign.

There is no doubt, either, that the abortion fight made Steel a national name. The press and public took more notice of what he said, although during the year in which he pushed the Bill through the Commons, he was in danger of becoming a 'one-issue' politician. He soon corrected that after the Bill became law by taking up other causes.

8

Steel and human rights

Jeremy Thorpe used to tell Liberal candidates fighting Conservative constituencies, 'Look right and talk left.' David Steel
neatly epitomises that advice. With his quiet, conservative
clothes, neat haircut and modest manner, he would not look out
of place in a trainload of commuters travelling home to Epsom.
Yet Steel has taken an uncompromising radical stance on a range
of human rights issues throughout his career. He has consistently
attacked racialism, backed liberation movements in the Third
World, especially Africa, and campaigned for more economic aid
and assistance for poorer nations.

Is this a paradox in Steel's political character? Beneath the
neatly tailored two-piece suits, is there a long-haired revolutionary with jeans and sloppy-joe sweater struggling to get
out? Steel certainly shares some, but not all, views of the various
protest movements of the late 1960s and the '70s. He opposes
racialism in every form, he is against a British independent
nuclear deterrent, (although he opposes independent nuclear
disarmament) and he wants ecological considerations given
greater weight in economic decisions.

Yet though he shares many of the same aims of these
movements, he disagrees with most of their campaign tactics. He
is at heart a parliamentarian, and believes that the parliamentary
system, suitably reformed, can be used to right most of the
wrongs in society today. You may see Steel on a protest march,
but he will be there because he feels a duty to support the
movement rather than because he feels it will achieve any
practical result.

You will not see Steel taking part in anything which smacks of
illegality or even irresponsibility. One of his first speeches as a
newly adopted Liberal candidate condemned the sit-down
demonstrations of the CND. Steel definitely does not like political
campaigners who paint on walls, throw things at politicians, dig

up sports pitches or disrupt lawful events.

When a smoke bomb was thrown at the South African Defence Minister Pieter Botha during an Anti-Apartheid Movement demonstration in Whitehall, Steel angrily wrote to the AAM to demand an explanation. If he had been told that smoke-bombing was on the agenda, he would not have attended, he said.

Steel opposes this kind of activity, partly on principle and partly on the grounds that it does not get the campaigners anywhere in the long run. Once again, we see the practical mind of Steel, the politician who wants results, at work. Steel says, 'Today's revolutionaries are open to suspicion. Abuse is always easier than discussion. Their theories are usually so stereotyped and removed from reality as to relieve them of any need for coherence or logic. They accentuate the negative and eliminate the positive.' Steel is certainly no darling of the revolutionary left, but he is well respected by a number of radically minded people in his own party, in other political parties, and outside politics altogether.

Race relations has become a major issue in British politics only in the last twenty years, the period during which Steel has been active as a politician. It first exploded onto the electoral scene in the 1964 general election in Smethwick, where, against national trends, a Conservative candidate defeated Labour's much-respected incumbent, Patrick Gordon Walker, after a campaign in which race and immigration played a prominent role. The issue continued to fester during the 1960s and early '70s, fanned by explosive speeches from Enoch Powell, and successive surrenders to racialism by Harold Wilson's government. During this period and during the 1970s, race relations have been complicated by Britain's attitude to South Africa, Rhodesia's illegal declaration of independence, and the racial policies of East African nations such as Kenya and Uganda. On all these issues, Steel has been quite outspoken.

But why should a Scottish MP from a rural constituency, in which there are practically no black inhabitants, be so deeply interested in such matters? And why should he consistently risk electoral unpopularity to take well-publicised stands? Steel is one of the few MPs in the House of Commons today who knows Africa at first hand. He went to Kenya as a schoolboy, and lived there for four years. His racially segregated school – whites only – made a deep impression on him, as did the blacks' struggle for independence. So did his father's support for the blacks' struggle.

To Steel, the belief that all men are created equal is rooted more in his religious than his political beliefs, the result of imbibing the egalitarian spirit of Scottish Presbyterianism at his father's knee from an early age. This is why, for Steel, the self-evident truth of the equality of the races is never a matter for compromise. He takes his text from the nineteenth-century Liberal philosopher John Stuart Mill: 'The inequality of rights has no other source than the law of the strongest. Was there ever any domination that did not appear natural to those who did not profess it? We ought not to ordain that to be born a girl instead of a boy, any more than to be born black instead of white, shall decide the person's position through all life.'

From 1966 to 1969 Steel was President of the Anti-Apartheid Movement in Britain. It was an important post for a young politician to hold. It brought further national attention to him, and gave him more experience of working with politicians in other parties to achieve shared objectives. The late 1960s were turbulent times for race relations in Britain. Enoch Powell stirred the pot with inflammatory speeches about race and immigration, and brought the subject into the centre of the political stage. Powell contended that Britain could not become a multi-racial society without creating unacceptable tensions within it. Steel strongly contested this view. He believed that Britain could absorb significant numbers of immigrants to whom previous British governments had given rights of entry, providing positive social and dispersal policies were adopted at the same time, similar to policies adopted by the Dutch to cope with their wave of immigration from the East Indies.

In 1968, the government, aided by the climate of public opinion created by Powell's speeches, introduced a bill to stop the flow of Asian immigrants from Kenya, where they were being persecuted by President Kenyatta's government. The government steamrollered the Bill through both Houses of Parliament in less than a week, unprecedented haste for a contentious measure, especially one affecting human rights. The Bill split the Labour and Conservative parties, and, once again, Steel found himself working with MPs from other parties in a common cause. With his detailed personal knowledge of Kenya, he made some effective interventions from the Liberal benches during the debates on

89

various stages of the Bill, which dragged on for a week almost all day and all night through both Houses of Parliament. Steel later wrote a book called *No Entry* (Christopher Hurst, London, 1969) about the episode and the background to it. He described the Commonwealth Immigrants Act 1968, as it was titled, as 'the most mischievous and misguided piece of legislation ever introduced into Parliament'.

Steel wrote the book, he said, 'not in order to cry over spilt milk, but in the hope that by detailing how and why it happened, we may avoid similar mistakes in the future.' He added that the way in which the Bill was railroaded through Parliament demonstrated that Britain needed a Bill of Rights as a 'second outer wall of defence around the liberty of the subject'.

When President Idi Amin started to expel Asians from Uganda in 1972, Edward Heath's Conservative government handled the sudden influx of refugees in a more humanitarian way. Steel was once again in the thick of the debate demanding that Britain should receive these people to whom Britain had given rights of citizenship and British passports.

In September of 1972, Steel, then Liberal chief whip, flew to Kampala to assess the situation personally. It was a visit not without some physical risk to himself. The Foreign Office urged him not to go. Relations between Britain and Uganda were strained, and only a week before Steel's departure Jeremy Thorpe, speaking to the Liberal assembly in Margate, had dubbed Amin a 'black Hitler'.

Steel flew into Entebbe from Nairobi on a practically empty DC9 of East African Airways. An official from the British High Commission met Steel, and his research assistant Archy Kirkwood, at the airport. On the drive into Kampala, their car was stopped twice at police and army road blocks. In Kampala, Steel found little evidence of a military presence. He visited a Kampala hospital in order to assess opinion from expatriates on the current situation. He met representatives of the British government's Uganda Resettlement Board, and spoke to some of the sixty refugees queueing up for entry visas outside the British High Commission. And he saw how the expulsion of the Asians had brought Kampala's commercial life close to a standstill. Steel roundly condemned Amin's policy.

Steel also took part in a highly publicised campaign against the

Wilson government's proposal to increase the fees of overseas students payable at British universities. Secretary of State for Education and Science Anthony Crosland wanted the fees raised from £70 a year to £250. Steel claimed the government risked losing much international goodwill for the relatively small saving of £5 million a year – 0.02 per cent of the annual defence budget. 'The rise will be particularly hard for underdeveloped countries at a time when Britain has cut her overseas aid expenditure. Yet aid in the form of subsidised education incurs no direct foreign exchange costs and seems the best we can afford during this balance of payments crisis.' Steel attacked the Labour government for failing to make any distinction between those who could and those who could not afford to pay the increases. 'A Texan oil millionaire's son pays the same as an Indian peasant's son. Is this Labour justice?'

Immigration and race relations are rarely big political issues in Steel's Roxburgh, Selkirk and Peebles constituency in the way in which they are in some inner city constituencies in England. When Steel's constituents complain about 'immigrants', they are usually talking about the English. This has made it easier from an electoral point of view for Steel to pursue this uncompromising stand on immigration and race relations.

However, although immigration is not a big issue in the Borders, rugby is. Borders rugby players frequently make up a substantial proportion of the Scotland Fifteen. In fact, rugby is little short of being a religion amongst some of Steel's voters. Although not a natural rugby fan himself – in fact, he takes little interest in any sports – Steel makes sure he turns out at important rugby fixtures in his constituency, and he occasionally turns up at Twickenham when Scotland is playing.

On the face of it, rugby has nothing to do with politics. But in early 1970, a proposal by the South African racially segregated Springbok rugby team to play in Steel's constituency at Galashiels created one of the greatest crises of conscience of his political career, and nearly cost him his seat. Steel has been a consistent critic of apartheid in South Africa. He opposes sporting links with South Africa, and dismisses the argument that the way to change the repugnant apartheid policy is to build links with South Africa. Steel points out that the admittedly small gains in integration in sport in South Africa have come about not by playing sport with

South Africa on their terms, but by excluding them from the international sporting community. As Steel puts it, 'There is no more feeble argument than "I disapprove of apartheid but ..." There can be no "buts" in the eyes of the majority of the people in South Africa or in the rest of the world. Sporting contacts have done nothing to alleviate apartheid. They have merely depressed those struggling against it.'

So Steel adamantly opposed the idea of a racially selected rugby team touring Britain in the winter of 1969–70. But with the prospect of the Springboks playing in Galashiels, to the delight of the majority of his rugby-loving constituents, Steel faced an uncomfortable choice. Should he personally campaign against the Springboks in his own constituency?

Steel clearly recognised that he would have to condemn the visit of the Springboks to his constituency, but how far should he go with his opposition? Could he conveniently absent himself from the constituency on the day of the match, and leave the protesting to others? Such tactics would have been an act of cowardice, and could well have backfired. He was a known opponent of apartheid. Not to have campaigned against it in his own backyard would have been construed by his political enemies as an act of political cowardice.

Steel's constituency association backed him. They passed a resolution condemning the match. Steel decided his tactics must be to condemn in unequivocal terms the Springboks' visit, but to distance himself from the kind of rent-a-mob protesters who might be attracted by the match. Steel set about carefully explaining his views to his constituents, while carefully disassociating himself from the more extreme and violent protesters who planned to invade rugby pitches and dig up the turf, tactics of which Steel definitely did not approve. Two days before the match, he organised a public meeting at Galashiels, and invited former Scottish Olympic athlete Menzies Campbell, a Scots sporting hero, to speak. The meeting was thinly attended by Borders' standards.

Steel told his constituents, 'The right to demonstrate is an important right enjoyed in this country – a right which does not exist in many countries in the world, including South Africa. Both nurses demonstrating for higher pay and opponents of apartheid demonstrating against the presence of a racially selected

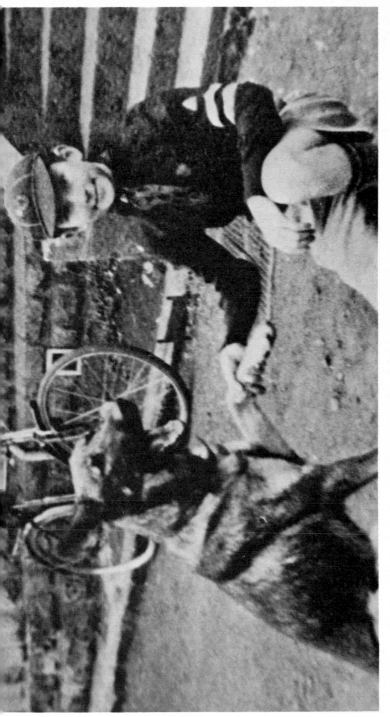

Aged twelve, in Wolf Cub uniform in Nairobi, with pet Alsation, Duke

Aged fifteen, with his younger brother and sisters

David Steel at the Edinburgh University rectorial installation of Jo Grimond, with actor James Robertson Justice (right)

Jubilant after his by-election win in 1965 at Roxburgh, Selkirk and Peebles

Family group, from left to right, Billy, Rory, Graeme, David, Catriona and Judy with pet Labrador, Jill

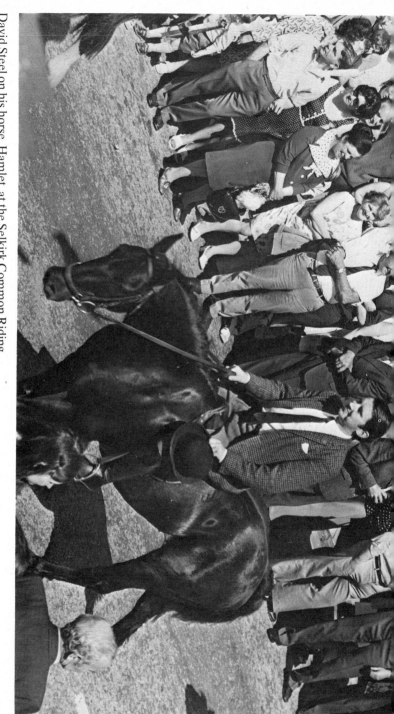

David Steel on his horse, Hamlet, at the Selkirk Common Riding

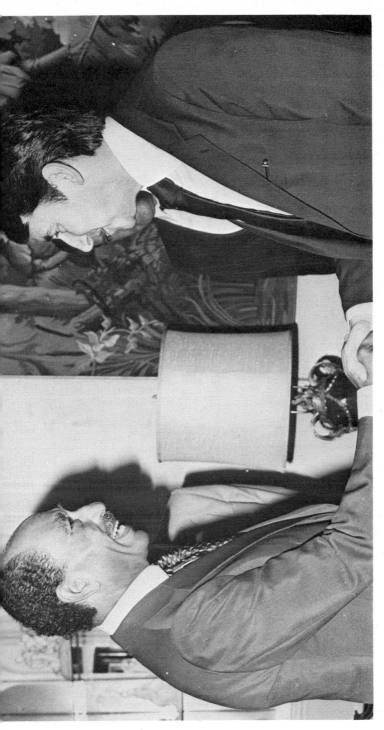

Meeting President Sadat in Cairo, in October 1980

In a relaxed mood

rugby team are entitled to attract public attention by this method.

'There is a danger, however, that the right to demonstrate may be brought into disrepute and even jeopardised by an irresponsible minority who indulge in disruption, violence or vandalism as part of their protest. They are no doubt as sincere as any other protesters, but they should bear in mind the damage they do to the cause they seek to support. Their activities are counter-productive in influencing public opinion and they forget the right of others to watch rugby, however offensive the selection of the teams may be.'

Steel agonised for several days over whether he should turn up at the demonstration outside the match. He and Judy discussed the problem for hours on end. They concluded that as he had campaigned vigorously against apartheid nationally, he could not duck the issue when it turned up on his own doorstep. He organised a demonstration outside the rugby ground in Galashiels on the day of the match. Local councillors, clergy and other supporters agreed to turn up for what Steel planned as an entirely peaceful protest. They planned to hand leaflets to people attending the match.

The night before the match was the first sleepless night Steel had had since he entered politics. Through those awful sleepless hours, two fears haunted him. What if his constituents should finally turn against him because of his opposition to the rugby tour? And what if his peaceful demonstration should be disrupted by more violent and militant protesters?

Saturday, 17 January 1970 was a rough day for David Steel. He encountered the first – and, incidentally, the last – real hatred he has ever had from his own constituents. He was spat at by some of his constituents, as he and his small band of demonstrators distributed 5,000 leaflets giving facts about apartheid to the rugby fans. Steel's worst fears were also realised. A chanting, banner-waving mob of protesters arrived from Glasgow. They stationed themselves close to Steel's small band and hurled insults at the four-deep lines of police and the arriving rugby fans. Fearing a violent confrontation, Steel persuaded them to leave when the match started, as his group planned to do. But unlike his group, which dispersed quietly, they marched four or five abreast into Galashiels, the wrong way round the one-way traffic system. Although Steel had played no part in their demonstration, he suffered from guilt by association. Hostility towards him from some of his constituents continued for several months. At the general election only five months later, the Conservatives did their best to revive the issue. On the eve of polling day, they distributed a leaflet throughout the constituency. It showed a pair of rugby goal posts, with a ball sailing between the uprights. The slogan on it: Convert to Conservatism. Many of Steel's constituents did just that. His majority slumped to 550, and he had to sit through a nail-biting recount at Jedburgh Town Hall.

Steel's re-election, like that of other Liberal candidates in the 1970 general election, was not helped by the tactics of the Young Liberals led by Peter Hain, who planned to disrupt Springbok cricket matches. Steel had been one of the first MPs to attack the Young Liberals' tactics, although he completely opposed the proposed Springbok tour. In a parliamentary debate, Steel had called the members of the Cricket Council 'frightened and worried' men for not cancelling their invitation to the South Africans in the face of massive protests. Steel had a special reason for opposing the tour, apart from his opposition on grounds of principle. The only Scottish match of the cricket tour was due to take place at Selkirk in his constituency. He was anxious to avoid a repetition of the acrimony over the rugby match.

For several years Peter Hain was the stormy petrel of the Liberal party. During this period, Steel was probably closer to him than any other Liberal MP. He maintained a kind of love-hate political relationship with Hain. He supported Hain's objectives, but did not always agree with his tactics. He was realistic enough to realise that Hain, a favourite *bête noire* of the Tory press, was an electoral liability to the Liberal party. Steel and Hain were good personal friends, and Hain was a guest at the Steel home in Ettrick Bridge. When Hain was charged with bank robbery, a charge which was comprehensively dismissed after a court hearing, Steel appeared in the witness box as a character witness for Hain. Steel did not join in the huge sigh of relief that went up from Liberal members when Hain quit the Liberal party to join Labour. He was angry with his colleague John Pardoe, who declared, 'for this relief, much thanks', when Hain left.

The search for a settlement in Rhodesia by successive British governments occupied much of Steel's early political career. Steel always backed the Liberal line that no settlement would be acceptable which was not based on a swift and steady progress towards majority rule. In October 1972, Steel flew to Rhodesia to find out first-hand the facts about the illegal regime, and to gauge African opinion.

He entered Rhodesia legally but quietly at Bulawayo. His passport, newly acquired for the trip, did not reveal that he was a Member of Parliament. At Bulawayo Airport, he encountered a dodge used by the Rhodesian authorities to aid sanctions busting. Instead of stamping his passport, the immigration official stamped a piece of cardboard which could be thrown away after Steel had left Rhodesia. When he visited other countries, his passport would contain no record that he had been in Rhodesia.

In Salisbury, Steel found there was still enough good will among the Africans and at least a section of the Europeans to make a settlement possible. Steel did not pass a harsh judgement on Rhodesia's whites. 'Salisbury has much the air of Nairobi as I knew it in pre-independence Kenya,' he said. 'The aged white settlers on the verandah of Meikle's Hotel look the same as those who lingered round the New Stanley twenty years ago. The Europeans of Rhodesia are not cruel or vicious people; their sin is a combination of greed and indifference. More than half of them are postwar immigrants, mainly from Britain, enjoying an artifically high standard of living which they want to hang on to.'

The visit to Rhodesia got Steel banned by the Smith regime. Immigration officers seized Steel at Salisbury Airport before his departure, searched his briefcase and copied several documents before returning them to him. They handed him a document making him a prohibited immigrant under the terms of Rhodesia's 1966 Immigration Act. Ian Smith claimed Steel had been banned because of his 'known support for terrorist movements'. But Steel said, 'I do not know what Mr Smith means by terrorist movements. I have never supported terrorism.' The ban was temporarily lifted by Bishop Muzorewa's provisional government, and finally abolished when Robert Mugabe came to power.

When a Rhodesian settlement was finally negotiated by Foreign Secretary Lord Carrington, Steel was generous with his praise for the achievement. But Steel has been very critical of the Thatcher government's record on foreign aid. He wants to see the recommendations of the Brandt Commission on the Third

World, which calls for much greater aid for underdeveloped countries, given more importance by Western governments. He believes that building economic, cultural and other links between nations is a way to end racial hatred. He once said, 'The breakdown in good relations between the races has in my view replaced the threat of nuclear war as the greatest danger facing mankind.'

9

Liberal locust years

An intriguing feature of Steel's political career is that its progress has been only partly allied to the fortunes of the Liberal party. This is especially true of the early part of his career, in the late 1960s and early 1970s. As the Liberal party's sun set, the Steel star rose higher in the political firmament. To understand why this should be so is to know more about him as a politician.

To begin with, Steel is a very untypical Liberal. Most Liberals are fascinated by the details of obscure policy proposals such as site value rating or proportional representation by the single transferable vote, proposals which seem so complex in operation that they defy the public to understand them. Steel is far less interested in the minutiae of policy than with developing the Liberal party as an effective voice and force in the British political landscape. Most Liberals measure the success of the Liberal party in terms of the triumph of Liberal candidates. Steel measures the success of the party in terms of the triumph of Liberal ideas. So whereas most Liberals are inward-looking, Steel is very definitely outward-looking.

It follows from this analysis that even when the party falls on hard times, a man with Steel's political outlook and temperament will seem of greater consequence in the big wide world than those who measure their contribution in purely party political terms. When the Liberal party does fall on hard times – and in the last twenty years those hard times have been more frequent than its brief periods of electoral prosperity – it becomes even more intensively inward-looking than usual. During these periods, the party spends more time contemplating its own navel than an Indian yogi. These navel contemplation sessions normally take the form of interminable reviews of the party's immensely complex constitution. Incredible though it may seem, there are Liberals who believe that the party's constitution is central to its political success.

The late 1960s was a period of deep introspection for the Liberal party, but one of considerable political experimentation and development for Steel. It was, essentially, a depressing period for radicals in British politics. The high hopes of British radicals, which had accompanied the election of Harold Wilson's government in 1964, had been cruelly dashed within two or three years. Successive economic crises reined back Labour's plans for bold social reform. The devaluation of the pound in 1968 was seen by many radicals as the ultimate sell-out to international financial interests. And, as we have seen, the government's record on immigration and race relations had disillusioned many of its supporters.

But in this political vacuum, the Liberal party failed to seize its electoral opportunity. The excitement of the election of Jeremy Thorpe as new Liberal leader soon fizzled out in the public mind. Thorpe's 'Great Crusade' to boost the Liberals' flagging fortunes and raise £1 million for party funds proved a damp squib. In by-elections, Liberal candidates lost a string of deposits in places as diverse as Acton, Dudley, Oldham West, Nelson and Colne, and Caerphilly. For all Thorpe's undoubted energy, the Liberal party lacked a defined and workable political strategy. Although Thorpe had backed Grimond's radical realignment policy, it somehow never featured as a big theme of the Thorpe leadership. Thorpe's speeches, while they were highly quotable and often amusing, lacked the broad philosophical sweep which Grimond had provided.

Steel, as we have seen, backed Thorpe for the leadership, and after the elction remained loyal to him. Yet while Steel dutifully played the role assigned to him by Thorpe – that of Commonwealth affairs spokesman in the House of Commons – he hankered after developing Grimond's views on radical realignment, which, to Steel, seemed even more relevant in the political climate of the late 1960s.

During this period, Steel was involved in a number of important and occasionally successful cross-party campaigns. His Abortion Act would never have been passed without the help of energetic young Labour Members and a handful of radical Tories. He was involved in many other campaigns fought on cross-party lines, such as those against the Commonwealth Immigrants Act and higher fees for overseas students. He held office in organisations such as the Anti-Apartheid Movement and Scottish Shelter, the housing charity and action group, which were not aligned with any particular political party. This provided him with a much wider experience than most young MPs get of working with like-minded people, whether from other political parties or outside the party system altogether. It was certainly an experience not shared by many of his political colleagues or many leading members of the Liberal party.

In early 1968, Steel, together with a small group of other leading Liberals, decided that the idea of radical realignment needed a sharp push, both inside and outside the Liberal party. They were stimulated by a gloomy editorial in *The Guardian* which said, 'Today's situation is one from which those who want a realignment on the left ought to profit. But they are not ready with a common policy or with the means to achieve a realignment. They are about to miss their chance again.'

Richard Holme, a Liberal candidate who had fought a by-election in East Grinstead, Sussex, at about the same time as Steel won his seat in Parliament, approached Steel with the idea for an organisation, containing Liberals but not part of the Liberal party, which would attract support from other radicals. They formed an organisation called the Radical Action Movement. Its other leading founders were John Pardoe, the Liberal MP for North Cornwall, Chris Layton, the perennially hopeful Liberal candidate for Chippenham, and Terry Lacey, a Young Liberal firebrand who later joined the Labour party.

The basic testament of RAM, as it became known, was a long wordy document full of phrases like 'the great questions of today', 'the legitimate needs and aspirations of the people', and a 'dialogue between the radical forces of Britain'. For Steel and the others, RAM was supposed to act as a 'catalyst of a much wider radical movement, and to start a debate both within the Labour and Liberal parties with the aim of forging an alliance between the progressive forces of Britain.' In other words, it was supposed to be a talking shop – but a talking shop with a difference. Whereas other pressure groups set themselves limited objectives, RAM wanted to break the political system of Britain and transform society. This seemed ambitious for an organisation with limited funds, run from Pardoe's home in Hampstead. Yet Steel threw himself enthusiastically into arguing RAM's case.

'Now the opportunity for political realignment is even greater outside Parliament than within. If the Liberal party can grasp the initiative in bringing this about, it deserves success,' said an early policy statement. RAM warned other Liberals, 'This may mean a reassessment of priorities, it may mean more militant attitudes, and it will certainly mean a greater awareness of the future than of the integrity of historical tradition.'

Steel also used his by now extensive contacts with other political radicals outside the Liberal party, to drum up support for RAM. He persuaded Peter Jackson, the Labour MP for High Peak, to sign up. Jackson had worked closely with Steel on the Abortion Bill. Steel also persuaded Labour MP Ben Whitaker (Hampstead), with whom he had worked closely in the Anti-Apartheid Movement, to join. This says something for Steel's power of persuasion, for RAM never looked more than a Liberal front organisation, and Labour MPs, under constant close surveillance by their whips, are traditionally nervous of joining such organisations. Steel also had a modest success in roping in some 'non-political' activists, such as Des Wilson from Shelter, Antony Steel from War on Want, and Lee Chapman from Oxfam. But despite this, RAM never developed any kind of mass membership and was treated with considerable suspicion by the rest of the Liberal party, even though Steel had very carefully assured everyone that RAM represented no threat to Jeremy Thorpe's leadership.

A year after its founding, Steel was still trying to breathe life into RAM by supporting Chris Layton's candidature in a Swindon by-election. 'We believe that a strong Liberal party can be a major force in any political changes that take place,' he said. And added significantly, 'The party label, however, is not really important; what we are looking for is any group of people that has a fresh, up-to-date approach to the problems of Britain.' When the votes were counted, Layton ended with a dismal 15 per cent of the poll, not enough to build RAM's political momentum, but just enough to reduce the Labour vote and hand the seat to the Conservatives. Nothing more was ever heard of RAM after this.

But the incident should not be written off in Steel's career as a failed political experiment. RAM convinced Steel that like-minded politicians could be brought to work together for something more than the limited objectives of an individual bill or a single issue pressure group. What were needed for success were the right political conditions, and a suitable power base to start the movement. Steel was convinced that a successful realignment could only take place if the Liberal party itself became the power base for a broader political grouping. And he firmly decided that if realignment were to be successful, there would first have to be a realignment of parliamentary forces before it could be truly effective at grass roots level in the country at large.

For the Liberal party as a whole, the 1970 general election switched the argument from realignment to survival. Traditionally, the Liberal party never does well at the end of a period of Labour government. In addition, the Liberals went into the campaign without any viable political strategy, a point Steel noted with concern. Jeremy Thorpe's effervescent style was no substitute for strategy, although he was always a popular and effective campaigner. The election theme, based on a manifesto entitled 'What a Life', was Thorpe's own, and Steel played no part in developing it and very little part in the national campaign. With the country polarised by an election, supporters of cross-party co-operation were thin on the ground.

Steel himself retreated to his Roxburgh, Selkirk and Peebles constituency to fight a grim rearguard action. As we have seen, his sponsorship of the Abortion Act and, more especially, his opposition to the Springboks' rugby tour in his own constituency had annoyed some of his constituents. The Springboks' tour had taken place in January, and the election came in June. Steel admits, 'If the election had come immediately afterwards, I think it would have been pretty fatal.' But the six-month interval helped him to mend some fences. He was helped by a former Roxburgh Labour candidate who wrote to the local papers saying that, although he was not a Liberal, he would vote for Steel because of the stand taken on this important issue. Even ardent rugby fans started to see there was a strong anti-apartheid case to be argued. Nevertheless, Steel says, 'It was very nasty canvassing during that election. That was the only election when there was hostility towards me.'

One factor helped Steel. He had been MP for the constituency for five years, and his constituents were beginning to see the benefits of having a Liberal MP. By 1970, depopulation in the Borders, which had been a big issue at the beginning of the 1960s, had been halted, largely as a result of positive government action. Steel's prodding and pushing of government ministers to provide aid for the Borders had been effective. His constituents could also see the after-effects of the last Conservative government. The most noticeable of these had been the closure of the railway line through the constituency, a delayed result of the Beeching Report on the railways – in fact, the line was actually closed by a Labour government.

Steel had been exceptionally active in his campaign against this decision, and it won him wide support amongst his constituents. He had cajoled local authorities in the Borders to commission an independent report on the viability of the Waverley rail line, which ran ninety-four miles from Edinburgh through the Borders to Carlisle. The report by transport economist John Hibbs, who later became a Liberal adviser on transport, concluded that part of the line running through Steel's constituency could be saved for a much lower subsidy than the government had suggested. Despite this, the government closed the line in January 1969. Steel rode on the last train through his constituency and addressed crowds of angry constituents who blocked the line and prevented the train from passing. This kind of parish pump action, later to be described by the phrase 'community politics', transformed Steel into something of a local hero.

Nevertheless, the 1970 election campaign in the Borders was the trickiest in which Steel had ever been involved. His new Conservative challenger, Russell Fairgrieve, a company director and chairman of the Scottish Wool Association, attacked Steel for allegedly wanting to break trade links with South Africa. 'Of all the constituencies in Scotland we would suffer most,' Fairgrieve told his audiences. 'We are proportionately large users of South Africa wools. South Africa is also a growth market for our knitwear and our tweed.' Steel hit back. He said he was 'definitely opposed' to demonstrations against Border firms doing business with South Africa.

An independent anti-abortion candidate claimed in a leaflet that Steel had been responsible through his abortion legislation for thirty-five and a half tons of aborted foetuses burnt in incinerators. In fact, this extremist presentation of an emotive issue may have aided Steel. People were revolted by it, and consequently sympathised with Steel. Besides, most of the

Catholics in Roxburgh proved to be of a fairly liberal disposition and, even if they did not approve of abortion, were prepared to accept that there might be another point of view.

On polling day, Steel scraped home with a 550-vote majority after two agonising recounts. That night was one of the blackest in recent Liberal history. More than half the parliamentary Liberal party lost their seats, including the indispensable Eric Lubbock, Liberal chief whip. A tiny drop in the party's share of the national poll, by about 1 per cent, had resulted in a loss of more than 50 per cent of its seats, once again demonstrating the ludicrous unfairness of the electoral system. Moreover, the Conservatives were returned to power with a comfortable majority, and any hope that the Liberals might exercise a pivotal position in the new Parliament was once again dashed.

After the election, the Liberal party seemed to suffer from shell shock. How could the work of a decade, painstakingly building up a parliamentary party into double figures, be wiped out in a single night, party faithful asked. In fact, although the election had been a disaster for the Liberals, parliamentary party survivors recognised that it had been a near catastrophe. 'The party came very much closer to being wiped out than most people think,' says Steel today. Three of the MPs, Thorpe, Pardoe and Steel himself, had clung to their seats with narrow three-figure majorities.

While Liberals all over the country beat their breasts and gnashed their teeth, Steel swiftly took stock of the situation. He had little doubt that the party had done badly nationally because it lacked a coherent political strategy. Within a few days of the election, at a victory rally in his Roxburgh constituency, Steel was suggesting that the party needed a new role. He wholly rejected the siren sounds from other parties suggesting the Liberals should submerge themselves in one of the larger parties. 'We must not see the country stranded with the straight jacket of only two parties each backed by their vested interests. We must continue to act as a stimulus, and if necessary an irritant, on the political scene,' he said.

But in an important development of his argument on realignment, he suggested that Liberal causes might not always be best served by backing Liberal candidates. 'My own view,' he said, 'is that possibly we should seek an entirely new role, less that of a conventional political party.' This unconventional role, in Steel's view, consisted of backing Liberal ideas wherever they were to be found. 'This may not necessarily mean putting up a Liberal candidate in every case.' Steel foresaw a situation where Liberals would back candidates from pressure groups like Shelter, Child Poverty Action or the Disablement Income Group because their aims were broadly sympathetic to Liberal policy.

Steel said, 'There is a growing fluidity in the political system. To say an MP is a Conservative tells me very little or nothing about his views on race, the Common Market or social services. To say a man is a member of the Labour party gives me equally little enlightenment. People are less and less inclined to support one political party right across the board on every policy. Liberals should seize the opportunities afforded by its fluidity to press Liberal principles and attract great public support. The party must be more than just a kind of Fabian Society with half a dozen seats in Parliament. It can use its organisation's strength wisely throughout Britain to promote its policies and see them adopted; not always by the direct means of nominating Liberal candidates – though that will remain the commonest method.'

This caused an instant furore in the Liberal party. It conflicted with the ideas of the majority of party activists, who believed that the primary duty of the party was to fight election campaigns. It set the scene for a vigorous debate at the Liberal assembly in Eastbourne three months later, in September.

On the eve of the assembly, Steel returned to his theme in a controversial article published in the *New Statesman*. This asserted that the Liberal party's radicals had to win a battle with the party's right wing – led, said Steel, by Emlyn Hooson, the MP for Montgomeryshire – before it could develop a lasting and successful political strategy. Steel bluntly accused Hooson of thwarting Jo Grimond's earlier attempts to promote a radical realignment. Steel asserted, 'There is still no more ludicrous proposition than that the Liberal party should be a party in the centre or "occupy the middle ground". The party must continue to declare itself as being on all the major issues – race, education, defence, constitutional reform, housing, social services, industrial relations – on the left of the dividing line between progress and reaction.' Steel said that Thorpe should be allowed to lead the party without constant sniping.

'The best step the party could take is to let Thorpe, as they never in the end let Jo Grimond, actually lead the party. The legion committees of deposit losers should be told by the assembly to leave the strategy to him and get on with their proper task of providing the ammunition. His task now is to lead a guerrilla band rather than a third party of the realm, a band concentrating on a few issues which will strike a response rather than posing as a shadow government with a policy for everything.'

And in language which was to be almost repeated in his first assembly speech as party leader six years later, he declared, 'It is worth having another attempt at creating a relevant Liberal party. Those unwilling to risk the discomfort of the journey would do better to get off the train now rather than spend their time pulling the communication cord once it is under way.'

Steel expressed these views with a new-found authority. After the election, he had been appointed chief whip in succession to Eric Lubbock, who had lost his seat at Orpington. This effectively made Steel number two in the Liberal party. This was underlined when Jeremy Thorpe bowed out of politics for two months following the tragic death of his wife Caroline in a motoring accident.

The Liberal assembly in Eastbourne that September was a gloomy affair held in the wake of a disastrous election result and Thorpe's personal tragedy. It was the most thinly attended assembly for years – most delegates had exhausted their holiday entitlement fighting the June general election and could not spare the time to attend. The only notable event of the assembly was a set-piece confrontation between Steel and John Pardoe over the future strategy of the party. Despite the election result, Pardoe was in a surprisingly bullish mood. He insisted that the Liberal party might be down, but not out, and he wanted the party to come out fighting with a determination to contest every seat at the next general election and every by-election in the intervening period. His fine tenor voice ringing round the half-empty Congress Theatre at Eastbourne brought cheers from the delegates and a standing ovation.

Steel then argued that the Pardoe plan was unrealistic. He said that the party had neither resources in men nor money to commit itself to fight on such a wide front. Steel said that a bad Liberal result was worse than no Liberal result, as it merely served to underline the party's weakness. He wanted the party to retrench its resources and concentrate on fighting those seats where it could do well, and he wanted more co-operation with other Liberal forces in politics. This debate clearly demonstrated a difference in style and approach between Pardoe and Steel, which was reflected in their leadership contest a few years later.

In the meantime, the Liberals could only look forward to reaping the electoral benefits of the mid-term unpopularity of the Tory government.

10

Revival – and decline

Early in 1972, David Steel sat down to write a letter which was eventually to have a significant effect on Liberal fortunes. The letter was addressed to Councillor Cyril Smith MBE, of Emma Street, Rochdale. Steel told Smith that Rochdale's Labour MP, Jack McCann, was far from well and that his untimely demise was quite possible. If this happened, would Smith fight the ensuing by-election for the Liberals?

Steel had never met Smith. He had, however, heard of Smith's reputation as a blunt, no-nonsense northerner who was already a household name in his home town of Rochdale. Smith's larger-than-life personality adequately matched his twenty-seven-stone bulk. Smith had originally joined the Liberals, defected to Labour and served as a councillor for several years, including one year as mayor, before switching back to the Liberals in 1968. In the 1970 general election, Smith had contested Rochdale as a Liberal candidate and hoisted the party's vote to 14,076 at a time when most other Liberal votes were falling. Rochdale had a long tradition of chapel Liberalism, and television personality Ludovic Kennedy had come within 3,000 votes of winning the seat in the 1959 general election.

As chief whip, Steel was responsible for the overall performance of Liberal candidates in parliamentary by-elections, hence his letter to Smith. Steel was convinced that, although there was no sign of a national swing to the Liberals, Smith's local popularity backed by a vigorous local campaign would capture the seat for the party and get the Liberal bandwagon rolling nationally.

The Liberals certainly needed some good news. After the terrible 1970 general election result, the party seemed to have lost its nerve. It became even more introspective than usual, and various sections of the party, such as the Young Liberals and Liberal Councillors, embarked on bad-tempered squabbles about future campaign tactics. These resulted in an acrimonious assembly at Scarborough in 1971, when Steel was called in to patch up a fight between the rebellious Young Liberals and the party leadership. The influential Association of Liberal Councillors had called for 'libertarian socialists and anarchists masquerading under the title of Young Liberals' to be booted out of the party. Young Liberal Chairman Peter Hain had asked Steel, as President of the Young Liberals, to intervene in order to cool the fury. However, Steel's role as President of the fractious Young Liberals earned him some sharp criticism from other members of the party, and the following year he did not seek re-election to that post.

Nor had by-elections been running the Liberal way, as they often do during periods of unpopular Tory government. The Liberal vote in most contests had remained fairly constant, and in some cases had even declined. Steel, incidentally, nearly lost his life when he went to speak at one of these by-election meetings at Shoreham in 1971. At Shoreham station he fell onto the railway line, missing fatal contact with the live rail by inches.

Cyril Smith politely declined Steel's invitation to fight Rochdale. But Steel would not take no for an answer. He wrote again. The answer was still no. But when McCann died later in the year, a highly persuasive telephone call from Jeremy Thorpe persuaded Smith to change his mind. Smith won the election with a 5,093 majority. This began one of the most spectacular Liberal revivals of the century. In just over a year, the Liberals won five by-elections, almost doubling the size of the parliamentary party. Steel played a significant role in most of these campaigns, especially at Sutton and Cheam, which was won in December 1972, and Berwick, which was won in 1973. At Sutton, Steel acted as a parliamentary liaison officer, keeping an eye on the harum scarum community politics campaign of Trevor 'Jones the Vote' Jones – the Liverpool-based election wonder-worker. Steel travelled weekly to Berwick after the resignation of Lord Lampton, the previous Tory MP, to hold an MP's surgery for the temporarily disenfranchised voters. As Liberal Alan Beith gained the seat with a wafer-thin majority of 34, Steel's intervention could well have proved decisive.

As chief whip, Steel's political stature grew noticeably during the 1970–4 Parliament. He firmly established himself as a respected political figure, and he remained a popular Member amongst other MPs. He was, however, the target of some criticism for his non-attendance at party committee meetings. Steel has always been impatient with the ponderous committee structure of the Liberal party, which seems to have been erected almost as a bar to effective decision-making and management of the party organisation. As chief whip, he held an *ex officio* seat on several of these bodies, but he was not a regular attender. Partly, this was because Steel represented a constituency some three hundred miles from Westminster and many of the committees held their meetings in London at the weekends, when Steel was involved in pressing constituency business and seeing his young family.

But there is no doubt that, along with Jeremy Thorpe, he was deeply disillusioned by the standard of leadership in the party outside Parliament. Steel often skipped meetings of the party's National Executive Committee. He says, 'There were one or two occasions when I was so appalled at the way they conducted business. They were just glorious talking shops with no sense of direction.' Since he became leader, Steel has had to mend his fences with the various organs of the party organisation in order to win broad-based backing in the party for his controversial leadership strategy. But he still makes little effort to conceal his impatience with the more impractical comments and proposals which emerge from party committees. As his former parliamentary aide Archy Kirkwood says, 'David does not suffer fools gladly, and since he became leader he suffers them even less gladly.'

As the winter of 1973–4 dragged on, and the miners' strike and the three-day week started to take their toll, Liberal support started to recede. When the general election was finally called by Ted Heath, Liberal support had sunk back to 11 per cent in the opinion polls, and many in the party predicted another disappointing general election result. The national campaign had, once again, been planned largely by Jeremy Thorpe, and Steel retired to his Roxburgh, Selkirk and Peebles constituency to defend his 550-vote majority.

In the event, the refreshing image presented by Jermey Thorpe of the Liberals as a party above the tired two-party class conflict of British politics caught the public imagination and Liberal support soared during the campaign. On polling day, the Liberals polled more than six million votes, their highest ever since universal suffrage was introduced, but won only fourteen seats. Steel scored a personal success by boosting his tiny majority to more than 9,000.

The election created a situation which was unique in British political history. Ted Heath's government lost its majority in the House of Commons, although it polled more votes in the country at large. Neither the first and third party nor the second and third party could command a majority in the House of Commons. Despite this, Heath did not resign immediately, but decided to explore the possibility of doing a parliamentary deal with the Liberals. The events of the four days following that election have been carved into Liberal mythology, and they were to colour deeply Steel's whole view about the practical problems of leading the Liberals into any parliamentary arrangement with another party.

The Saturday after polling day, a Heath aide telephoned Thorpe at his cottage Higher Chuggaton, in north Devon and asked him to visit Downing Street for a meeting with the Prime Minister. Thorpe caught the morning express from Taunton for an afternoon meeting in town. By the time the train pulled into Paddington, news of Heath's invitation had leaked out, and was the lead story in radio news bulletins. Thorpe had not thought to telephone any of his colleagues to inform them of Heath's invitation before rushing for the Taunton train. So Steel, number two in the parliamentary party and, as chief whip, the link with the party organisation in the country, heard about it on his car radio as he drove around his constituency on his traditional thank-you tour. 'This was certainly somewhat unusual,' he says.

Later on Saturday afternoon, Steel contacted Thorpe at his London home in Orme Square. He discussed Heath's approach and arranged to travel to London the next day (Sunday) for a fuller discussion. By now, Liberal workers all over the country had also heard the news and Steel's phone started ringing, as outraged members called to protest about what they saw as an incipient deal with the defeated Tories. The constant stream of phone calls shattered the peace of Steel's Saturday evening, and his patience steadily got shorter with the callers. 'What was disconcerting,' says Steel, 'was the number of time-consuming telephone calls we received, together with letters and telegrams, which told us what we knew already.' This was that there was never a chance of a deal with the Tories, unless Heath could offer a copper-bottomed guarantee to introduce proportional representation.

On Sunday, a small group of Liberals, consisting of Steel, Jo Grimond and Lord Byers, the Liberals' elder statesman, met at Thorpe's Orme Square home for lunch. Over the roast beef, they discussed Heath's offer in detail. The meeting came out very strongly against any deal with Heath, and Steel agreed with this. Steel says, 'I took that view from the moment I left my constituency, because it had been quite clear from my own constituency association that they were quite opposed to propping up Heath's government.'

The following day, the new parliamentary party discussed the Heath offer. They were unanimously against accepting any arrangement with the Tories unless proportional representation was definitely on offer. During the meeting, a messenger arrived from Heath carrying a letter which made it clear that the Conservatives would offer no more than a Speaker's conference on electoral reform, not enough to satisfy the Liberals. From that moment, the parliamentary Liberal party knew the coalition offer was a non-starter. This might have been a personal disappointment to senior Liberal parliamentarians, for Thorpe had been offered a senior post with a seat in the cabinet, and it is reasonable to assume that Steel would have received a senior ministerial post outside the cabinet.

Although the parliamentary Liberal party had been unanimous in rejecting the Heath offer, its discussion had disclosed a worrying split to Steel. He had argued in the meeting that, while it was correct to reject this coalition offer because the terms and conditions were not right, it would be wrong to rule out any idea of a coalition in the future. He says, 'I remember feeling very strongly in the full parliamentary party discussion that we had on Monday that it was one thing to say this was not the right thing to do, but quite another to advance the general argument, which a lot of people in the party did, that under no circumstances should anything like this be contemplated.'

Steel says, 'It seemed to me that these were two entirely different propositions. I was certainly against the Heath deal for a

111

whole variety of reasons – the fact that there wasn't a parliamentary majority, the fact that Heath had been refused a mandate by the country, and that we had got a big vote against him. We could hardly then be seen to go and prop up a Prime Minister who had lost an election on his own accord. But that was very different from saying that it was wicked to say that the party should ever contemplate a coalition. I found that very worrying.' Significantly, only two other members of the parliamentary Liberal party also expressed the view that it was not wrong in itself to have these discussions – Grimond and Russell Johnston, the MP for Inverness.

After the meeting, Steel drove Thorpe round to Downing Street, where Heath was told that as far as the Liberals were concerned there was nothing doing. Steel sat outside in the car while Thorpe went in to end the Conservative administration.

For the Liberal party, the period between the February and October 1974 general elections was a curious mixture of euphoria and trauma. There was euphoria at the party's quite unexpected and brilliant success at polling six million votes. But the hung Parliament and the implications this had for a possible Liberal role in a coalition government caused some traumatic heart-searching in the party. As the months between the February and October elections wore on, Steel became increasingly alarmed at the failure of Liberals at every level in the party to face up to the coalition issue.

After the February election, a period of what might be termed controlled anarchy broke out amongst Liberals, as the various organs of the party pontificated on the correct strategy for the Liberals to adopt in their changed circumstances. Many of the more optimistic Liberals wanted nothing less than a flat-out campaign for Liberal power at the next election. They believed that if the party could hoist its national poll to nine million votes or more, they would achieve a 'total breakthrough' and the electoral system, which normally worked against the Liberals, would start working in their favour. They coined the slogan 'One more heave' to encourage voters to believe that another mighty effort could bring a majority Liberal government.

The more sober members of the parliamentary Liberal party, most notably Steel, felt that optimistic talk about a Liberal government was no substitute for a viable electoral strategy in

Britain's confused political climate. Steel wanted the Liberals to play the coalition card quite bluntly and make a virtue of necessity. He believed that the mood in the country was turning against one-party governments, with the confrontationist policies they implied, and that a Liberal appeal to be part of a more broadly based government, rather than for a majority of its own, would strike a chord with voters who wanted fair play and common sense.

One of the prerogatives of the chief whip is to schedule the Liberals' party political broadcasts. The Liberals were due for a broadcast in late June, and Steel decided, after consultation with Thorpe and other leading Liberals, to make it himself. He decided that the coalition argument ought to be deployed forcefully in the broadcast. Without consulting any other members of the party, either inside or outside Parliament, Steel drafted his own script for the broadcast. Before leaving for the television studios to record the broadcast he dropped off a copy of his speech at Thorpe's office.

Thorpe read the script with some concern. He agreed with the basic thinking behind Steel's coalition arguments, but was deeply concerned that Steel's very frank presentation of the case, with no holds barred, would infuriate Liberal activists throughout the country. Just before Steel was due to start recording the broadcast, Thorpe telephoned. He asked for some amendments to the script designed to tone down the argument, and after a brief and friendly discussion, Steel agreed. Nevertheless, what Steel said that night, sent a shiver of alarm through the other parties, and plunged the Liberals into a furious argument about their own political strategy.

Steel argued that the fight against inflation could not be successfully waged by a government based on one party and narrowly appealing to one sectional interest in the community. He said, 'In our crisis we surely need a much more broadly based government backed by a real majority of public opinion, and that means that all parties must be willing to come together on an agreed programme in the national interest. I find the public demand for a government of national unity is now gaining considerably more force, but it can only come about if we get more Liberals in Parliament.'

Steel went on: 'We are ready and willing to participate in such

113

a government if at the next election you give us the power to do so. Naturally, like the other parties, we would prefer you to give us an overall majority of seats, but if you don't, we remain ready to contribute towards the kind of fair government based on partnership which you, the electorate, might be seeking. Any party which refused to consider this would be seeking to put power for their own party before the will of the people.'

He then explained why the Liberals had not entered a coalition with Heath's government, and concluded: 'The pattern of the two-party strangehold on British politics is breaking up. That has not been achieved by politicians; you have done it. You have decided rightly that it must end. And what we Liberals ask of you now is that at the next election, whenever it comes, you give us sufficient Members of Parliament to ensure the end of the system of one-party government, which has failed in recent years to unite the nation and give our country the kind of reforming government which represents the wishes of a clear majority of our people and which alone will therefore have the capacity to solve our problems.'

Just four days later, the Liberal party's National Executive Committee, which mostly consists of people who have failed to win elections, repudiated Steel's policy. They passed a resolution that 'the Liberal party will not join a coalition with the Conservative or Labour parties separately and will make this clear at the next election.' This did not rule out a government of national unity, comprising all parties, but it fell far short of the positive commitment to coalition that Steel wanted. He bluntly told the Executive members that their resolution was worthless. 'The decision on whether the circumstances and terms are right for Liberal participation in any government will be a matter for the enlarged parliamentary party. That is why the present parliamentary party has not committed us to any firm directions prior to the election and why the Executive decision to rule out options can have no validity.'

Today Steel says, 'Possibly it was rash at the time to make that broadcast and it did lead to criticism. But it did have its effect. It got a lot of attention.' One of its effects was finally to persuade rebel Labour MP Christopher Mayhew to quit his party and join the Liberals. Steel believes the broadcast created the right climate in which he finally decided to make his move.

There is little doubt now that Steel had correctly caught the tide of public opinion. The Liberal share in opinion polls jumped immediately after the broadcast. Market research secretly conducted by the Conservative party revealed that the public yearned for a political approach which stressed unity rather than divisiveness, and Heath made the idea of bringing non-Conservatives into a Tory-based government a theme of his autumn election campaign, thus considerably blunting what could have been a unique and effective Liberal appeal.

By the election, the Liberal party's leadership had substantially retreated from the forthright position Steel had spelled out in his party political broadcast. In two speeches at the assembly, Thorpe said that Liberals would campaign for an overall majority, but if denied it, would accept in exceptional circumstances participation in a more broadly based government. Steel sharply disagreed with Thorpe's desire to soft-soap the assembly. He believed the issue should have been met head on and debated, as this could have provided the Liberals with a much more viable election strategy. Steel says, 'I think it was a missed opportunity, and I think the October 1974 election was a missed opportunity because we should have adopted a coalition strategy. It might have caught on. I disagreed at the time with that strategy, and thought the party had really flunked the issue of participation in government as a means of getting more Liberals into Parliament.'

During the national campaign, Steel played a small role by heading a publicity committee together with Lord Avebury. But the committee was formed only shortly before the election, and it had hardly any time to start work before the election was called. Steel comfortably retained his seat in Roxburgh although his majority was down from 9,000 to about 7,000. Harold Wilson's government was returned with a small majority, and for the time being the role of the Liberals in Parliament became less important again.

Shortly after Parliament had reassembled, Steel decided it was time to stand down as chief whip. The suggestion that he should give up the job came from his original political mentor, Jo Grimond. During a fatherly chat, Grimond pointed out that the job of chief whip, which tied its holder very closely to Parliament, was politically limiting. Steel was still young, said Grimond, and should broaden his political horizons.

Steel had, in any event, been feeling the need for a change. He wanted to resign after the February election, but Thorpe persuaded him to stay on during the short Parliament. Steel was out of sympathy with the strategy the party adopted to fight the election and felt that it had consequently missed an opportunity. Besides, he was tired of being the peacemaker in the parliamentary party. In the previous year or so, there had been many internal eruptions in the parliamentary party, often caused by Thorpe's patrician style of leadership. Steel had played a key role in smoothing over these problems, but it was an exhausting and thankless task. Steel had been a good chief whip for Thorpe, and there was an excellent rapport between the two, although Steel's relations with the party organisation had been less cosy. Steel says, 'I found the job increasingly a tie and a chore, and there was a need for someone fresh in that role who would spend more time liaising with the party organisation and getting more involved with the party machine than I was prepared to.'

Although Steel wanted to quit the job straight away, Thorpe asked him to carry on for the time being. It needed a major row in the parliamentary party sparked off by John Pardoe before Steel was finally allowed to stand down, to be replaced by Cyril Smith.

Steel became the Liberals' Foreign Office spokesman, and increasingly spent more of his time on European and African affairs. He was the main Liberal representative on the Executive Committee of the Britain in Europe campaign during the 1975 referendum on Britain's continuing membership, when he worked closely with Roy Jenkins and politicians in other parties in the kind of cross-party campaigning at which he had become especially adept.

However, Steel had hardly time to settle into his new job before what some newspapers referred to as the greatest political scandal of the twentieth century engulfed the Liberal party.

11

Steel for leader

On 26 May 1971, an elderly lady and a young man arrived at the House of Commons. They walked across the ornate central lobby to the desk where the public ask to see their Members of Parliament. The attendant on the desk took their names, and asked which MP they wanted to see. In due course, a secretary came and escorted them to the MP's office. That MP was David Steel. The elderly lady was called Mrs Gwen Parry-Jones, and the young man Norman Scott. The story they were about to tell Steel was eventually to create a major scandal and lead to the downfall of Jeremy Thorpe as leader of the Liberal party.

Mrs Parry-Jones and Scott had, in fact, come to see Emlyn Hooson, the MP for Montgomeryshire, but Hooson had been called away to an important legal conference – he is an eminent QC – and Steel, as Liberal chief whip, had agreed to sit in on the meeting for him. Mrs Parry-Jones, a keen Liberal supporter from Talybont, Dyfed, had originally written to Hooson because he was Liberal MP for the neighbouring constituency. She had befriended Scott, then living in Talybont, who had made various allegations against a Liberal MP. In her letter to Hooson, she had suggested that these ought to be looked into by the Liberal party, as Scott seemed to have been rather badly treated. Hooson, deeply worried, had shown this letter to Steel, so it was appropriate that he should see Mrs Parry-Jones and Scott in Hooson's absence.

His two visitors were shown into Steel's room, the chief whip's office, just off the Members's lobby. Mrs Parry-Jones explained how she had come to know Scott, while Scott sat nervously fidgeting on his seat. Steel, who is normally good at making snap judgements about people, felt Mrs Parry-Jones was a kind and responsible person. He thought Scott looked like a person who lived on his nerves. Scott's story considerably shocked Steel.

His allegations, which have been extensively chronicled elsewhere (for example, in *Jeremy Thorpe – a secret life*, by

Chester, Linklater & May, published by Andre Deutsch, London, 1979), related to a claimed homosexual relationship with an MP. The punch line came when Scott revealed that the MP was Jeremy Thorpe. Hooson had presumed that the allegations related to Peter Bessell, the former MP for Bodmin, who had stood down at the previous general election. The news momentarily poleaxed Steel, but he consoled himself with the thought that Scott hardly seemed a reliable person. Scott produced a bundle of letters which purported to prove his allegations. Grim-faced, Steel flipped through these and noticed that they had all been written by Bessell to Scott. Most of them were letters which had accompanied small payments that Bessell had made to Scott over a period of a few years in the late 1960s. Only one of the letters actually mentioned Thorpe, and that was far from conclusive.

Steel, it is sometimes forgotten, trained as a lawyer, although he has never practised the law professionally. He has, however, a lawyer's instincts, and in this case his instinct was to test the validity of the allegations which Scott had made. He asked Scott to stay in London for a few days while he consulted with colleagues. Steel said he would like to see Scott again when these consultations had taken place.

The next day Steel went to see Hooson. He told him about Scott's allegations, and the two decided that Scott must be more closely questioned on his story. Scott came to the House of Commons the next day, and at the end of a lengthy session Steel remained in two minds about Scott's allegations. He felt that Scott's allegations must be unreliable in the absence of convincing corroborative evidence, but at the same time felt that they were so serious that they could not just be dismissed as the ravings of a crank. He was also very worried that to pursue these enquiries could be construed as disloyalty to his leader.

In the event, a further investigation of Scott's story was precipitated by a telephone call between Hooson and Bessell. Bessell admitted that there had been a problem with Norman Scott. Hooson bluntly told Bessell that in that case Thorpe would have to resign, and announced that he planned to ask Steel, as chief whip, to call a meeting of the parliamentary party to discuss the affair. The threatened meeting never took place, for Thorpe returned from an extended visit to Africa the next day and was immediately briefed by Bessell on the latest developments. This led to a strained meeting in Thorpe's room at the House of Commons a day later, during which both Steel and Hooson confronted Thorpe with the allegations. Thorpe was in a bitter and angry mood, and suspected that Hooson wanted to get rid of him as leader so that he could make another bid for the leadership himself. It was Steel, with his cool yet firm approach, who calmed Thorpe down.

Gently but firmly, Steel told Thorpe that the allegations laid him open to blackmail. There must be an enquiry, Steel said, if only to clear the air. He pointed out that the enquiry could be conducted very privately by the party itself, so that there were no leaks to the press. Reluctantly Thorpe agreed to this, but asked that Lord Byers, the Liberal leader in the House of Lords, should chair it. The other members of the enquiry team were Steel and Hooson.

During the next few days, Steel and Hooson gathered what evidence they could about Scott, and the bizarre story he had to tell. Scott claimed that he had had a homosexual relationship with Jeremy Thorpe which had started in 1961 – six years before the Sexual Offences Act was passed relaxing some of the restrictions against homosexuality. Thorpe has always strenuously denied this. Steel telephoned Scott's mother, who lived in Kent, and discussed the allegations with her. She confirmed her son's story, but could add no convincing evidence. Meanwhile, Hooson had tracked down a Detective Inspector Smith, a police officer based in Chelsea, who had interviewed Scott some years earlier in connection with allegations against Thorpe. Smith said he would be prepared to answer questions from the Liberal enquiry about the police investigation of Thorpe back in 1962.

Just thirteen days after Scott first walked into Steel's office at the House of Commons, the enquiry gathered in Byers' room at the House of Lords. It was a tense and unhappy meeting, with Scott whining about his alleged ill-treatment at the hands of Thorpe. Uncomfortably, Steel found himself the man in the middle between Byers, who took a hostile attitude towards Scott, and Hooson, who adopted a more conciliatory tone. Byers did most of the talking, and the meeting ended with Scott storming out in a huff after Byers had accused him of blackmail. The following day, the enquiry team saw Detective Inspector Smith, who was accompanied by a more senior officer. This meeting was also inconclusive, as the police refused to produce the statement which Scott had made in 1962. The officers did, however, indicate that no prosecution had been brought because there had been insufficient evidence. This point influenced Steel to believe that the allegations against Thorpe ought to be dismissed as unproven. In any event, in the absence of any evidence from a third source, Steel had to believe either the story told by Scott or Thorpe's version of events. And Scott was clearly a man in whom one could repose little trust.

After the 1971 enquiry, with its inconclusive result, Steel heard no more about the Scott affair for several years. However, the affair simmered away within the Liberal party, with Thorpe making desperate efforts to keep the matter secret. Steel knew nothing about the increasingly frantic attempts to keep the lid on the Scott affair until early 1976. By then, he had been succeeded by Cyril Smith as Liberal chief whip. Early in January a worried Smith approached Steel. Thorpe had just told Smith about the 1971 enquiry, and he wanted to know more about it. Scott was due to appear in a court case in Devon involving an airline pilot, Andrew Newton, who had shot Scott's dog and was to be tried for illegal possession of a firearm. Thorpe had told Smith that Scott would allege, in the privilege of the courtroom, that he had had a homosexual relationship with him. He added that Scott had a record of psychiatric illness, and that it might be useful if this information were passed on to the Home Secretary, Roy Jenkins, as the police were still conducting an investigation and ought to have all relevant information.

Steel, who knew Jenkins reasonably well from the days when he piloted his Abortion Act through Parliament, agreed to go with Smith to see the Home Secretary. Jenkins agreed to provide the police with the information about Scott's background, but firmly stated that he could not interfere in the inquiry.

The dam burst on the Thorpe affair quicker than expected. On 29 January 1976, before the Newton case came to court, Scott appeared at Barnstaple magistrates court charged with defrauding the Department of Health and Social Security of benefit money. During the hearing, he made his sensational statement, that he was being 'hounded by people' because he had once had a homosexual relationship with Thorpe. The story at once hit the newspaper headlines, and although Thorpe issued a clear and categorical denial of Scott's allegations, during the next few months further investigations by reporters revealed a complex and, at times, bizarre web of activities surrounding the relationship between Thorpe and Scott.

The next few months was a hellish period for the Liberal party and for Steel. He had always been an ardent Thorpe man. It is arguable that Thorpe partly owed his election as leader of the party to Steel who campaigned so vigorously on his behalf amongst other members of the parliamentary Liberal party. Steel remained a close political, although not personal, confidant of Thorpe. And although Steel and Thorpe are completely different in character, there was much about Thorpe as a politician that Steel could admire, especially his unflinching radicalism and concern for human rights.

As the Thorpe saga developed, with fresh revelations, Steel found himself shocked, and at times revolted, by the allegations. He also found his sense of loyalty tested, for Steel is an intensely loyal person. He felt a deep sense of loyalty to Thorpe, but he also had a deeper loyalty to the Liberal party, and in the end it was this second loyalty which was to prevail. However, Steel is also a very fair man and, unlike some other members of the parliamentary Liberal party, he did not rush to condemn Thorpe. A few days after Scott's courtroom outburst, the parliamentary party met to discuss the allegations against Thorpe. It was one of the most unpleasant meetings which the parliamentary party has ever held. Thorpe denied the allegations against him, but other members were sceptical about the way he had handled the affair. By now, Steel had increasing doubts about Thorpe's conduct, but he was still not prepared to condemn him. Steel's legal training still told him that the evidence was far from conclusive, and that Thorpe could not be condemned on the wild statements of a man he personally judged to be unstable.

The straw that finally broke Steel's back came on 5 March 1976, when David Holmes, Thorpe's close friend, issued a statement through his solicitor, to the effect that he had supplied the funds which had been used to buy a collection of letters written to Scott by Bessell and said to contain damaging references to Thorpe. Although the purchase of these letters had already become public knowledge, the source of the £2,500 used to buy them had been a matter of intense speculation.

Steel found it hard to believe that the purchase of these letters by Holmes, who had been best man at Thorpe's first wedding and was godfather to his son, could not have taken place without Thorpe's knowledge. This meant that Thorpe had not been entirely frank either with him or with the rest of the parliamentary party, and effectively undermined the credibility of the rest of Thorpe's story. A few days later, Steel met Thorpe at the House of Commons, and in a private conversation told him in a blunt but friendly way that it was time to step down as leader of the party. It is possible that from this meeting, Thorpe knew that his time as Liberal leader was now running out. The support of Steel, a pivotal and influential individual in the parliamentary Liberal party, was essential to Thorpe's continuing leadership.

Steel then learnt that the £2,500 had come from a secret fund whose existence was unknown to him or anyone else in the Liberal party. The fund passed through a bank account in the Channel Islands. It reinforced his view that the time had come for Thorpe to quit.

Although Thorpe still clung to some last hopes that somehow he might weather the storm, the practical Steel knew by now that his period as leader could not last much longer, and he anticipated the political situation which would arise in the Liberal party as a result of Thorpe's departure. Unlike the occasions when Grimond and Thorpe became leaders, there was no obvious heir apparent, but Steel realistically assessed that he might be a candidate for the leadership, although he had no strong desire at this stage to lead the party in the immediate aftermath of the Thorpe affair. Steel also felt that John Pardoe, the MP for North Cornwall, would be a likely candidate.

In view of this, Steel approached Pardoe privately to discuss the succession. Both men were acutely aware that leading the party in the aftermath of the Thorpe affair would be exceedingly difficult. They were also anxious to avoid a bruising electoral contest which could further harm morale in an already shell-shocked party. This point was especially important in view of the fact that the party had not completed the review of its constitution then in progress and had therefore not yet adopted the promised new method of electing the party leader which would give more influence to the rank-and-file members. The two men had a sombre discussion about the party's prospects. They concluded that the party needed a figure around whom all could unite at this difficult time. There was only one man in the party who fitted this exacting job description, and that was the Liberals' former leader Jo Grimond.

Secretly, Steel and Pardoe approached Grimond to ask him to return for another extended period as leader when Thorpe finally quit. Grimond listened to the persuasive arguments they deployed, but firmly declined their suggestion.

The beginning of the end for Jeremy Thorpe came on 9 May, when the *Sunday Times* printed the text of a letter sent by Thorpe to Scott. The letter had been signed, 'Yours affectionately Jeremy' and contained the widely quoted sentence, 'Bunnies can and will go to France.' The letter had a PS: 'I miss you.'

That weekend, Thorpe had travelled to the Suffolk home of Clement Freud, the gourmet, and Liberal MP for the Isle of Ely. Freud remained totally loyal to Thorpe, but with the candour of a true friend explained, two months after Steel and in similar terms, that for the good of the party and himself, it really was time to stand down as leader. As Thorpe mulled over the headlines in the *Sunday Times*, he reluctantly agreed.

Freud immediately telephoned Steel at his Ettrick Bridge home. Although Steel was no longer chief whip, he was, in fact, standing in for Alan Beith, who was abroad and temporarily absent from his post. Steel took Freud's phone call with a profound sense of relief, and agreed to travel south later that day for a meeting at Freud's London home on Monday morning. The meeting next day was cool, and not without sadness all round. Thorpe repeated his intention to resign, and the three sat about discussing the exchange of letters which would be made public later that day. In his resignation letter, which was addressed to Steel, Thorpe said, 'No man can effectively lead a party if the greater part of his time has to be devoted to answering allegations as they arise and countering continuing plots and intrigue.' The letter was signed, 'Yours affectionately, Jeremy'.

Steel replied with a letter which was fulsome in its praise for Thorpe's work. He said, 'Your personal qualities of leadership, charisma and sheer perseverance and your triumphs over adversity are held in the highest regard by all your colleagues and admired by the public at large. Your selfless decision to stand down now in the interest of the party is characteristic. I am glad that you are remaining with us as a parliamentary colleague. You will be greatly sustained in the months ahead by your constituents as well as your family, and we all look forward to a time when, freed of your present troubles, you return to a key role in the public life of our country.' The letter was signed, 'Yours affectionately, David'. This letter might have been less fulsome in its praise had Steel known of the intrigue and financial dealings in the Thorpe saga, later to be revealed.

Thorpe's resignation threw the Liberal party into alarm and confusion. It had been intended that the party should adopt a new procedure for electing a leader at its forthcoming assembly in September – still four months away. The party could not remain leaderless for that time, yet for the parliamentary party to conduct its own election without reference to the wishes of ordinary party members could only lead to a further furore, the last thing Liberals wanted at this time.

Steel and Pardoe approached Grimond again to see if he would take on the leadership temporarily until a new method of electing the leader had been agreed. Grimond was not happy about the idea, but for the sake of the party agreed – but only on the strict understanding that the new rules should be agreed as expeditiously as possible, and that the election take place immediately thereafter. The new rules were, in fact, adopted at a surprisingly optimistic and well-run special Liberal assembly held in Manchester in early June and attended by 1,500 delegates. The rules provided for candidates to be MPs and nominated by at least one fifth of the parliamentary party. Every paid-up Liberal member could then vote for the candidate of his choice in his own constituency. Each constituency had been allocated a number of 'national votes' depending on the size of the Liberal vote in that constituency at the last election – the larger the election vote, the more national votes it got. The votes of Liberal members were then counted constituency by constituency. The national votes were then allocated to each candidate in each constituency in direct proportion to the members' votes.

Although Pardoe had declared his candidature immediately, Steel waited until he had had a chance to discuss the subject with his family and constituency officers. Steel's wife was unhappy about his standing, feeling that it might take him away from home even more than at present. But in the end, she agreed that it would be the right thing to do for his career and the party. The key constituency officers also discussed the implications of their MP being party leader. They agreed they could shoulder the extra burden this would involve. In matters affecting his constituency, Steel is particularly influenced by Andrew Haddon, a wise old solicitor. Haddon has been President of Roxburgh, Selkirk and Peebles Liberals for many years, and he urged Steel to stand.

Steel tossed his hat into the ring at a meeting in Hampstead on 18 May. His speech reiterated his by now well-established views on realignment politics. The speech clearly defined the kind of direction Steel would move the party. He said that the Liberals should not act like a shadow third government waiting in the wings. The party's role, as Steel saw it, was to 'spell out a clear vision of the society we want to achieve; to provide long-term goals to people weary of the politics of pragmatism, expediency and compromise'.

He said, 'We must concentrate less on giving day-to-day commentary on the policies of others, and far more on setting out our own programme. And we should combine our long-term programme with a readiness to work with others wherever we see what Jo Grimond has called the break in the clouds – the chance to implement any of our Liberal policies.' Steel reminded his audience that he had worked with people from other parties on such issues as membership of the EEC, anti-apartheid, legislation on social reforms, housing, devolution and electoral reform. 'The experience has not made me any less of a Liberal, nor comprised the independence of Liberalism.'

Steel concluded his speech by developing Harry Truman's well-worn aphorism, 'If you can't stand the heat, get out of the kitchen.' He said, 'In these days it has been put to me bluntly that if you find yourself in the kitchen anyway, you might as well take charge of the menu.' The speech was short on specific policy proposals, although these had been covered in a pamphlet written by Steel the previous year called *Strategy 2000*. This pamphlet, described by the *Daily Telegraph* as 'a rich and gaudy miscellany of improbable suggestions', demanded a year's civil or military national service in return for larger student grants, the forced sale of council houses by converting rents to mortgage repayments, a statutory prices and incomes policy, and no social security benefits for strikers' families if the strike was approved by less than 50 per cent of the strikers in a secret ballot. The pamphlet also prophetically looked ahead to an alliance with the Social Democrats. Steel said – and this was years before the Social Democrats quit the Labour party – 'Many of the self-styled social democrats [in the Labour party] would be in happier company in combination with Liberals than socialists. Should such an opportunity for an effective regrouping of the left come about, it is important that the Liberal party should not behave like a more rigid sect of the Exclusive Brethren, but should be ready to join with others in the more effective promotion of liberalism.'

When nominations closed, the fight for the leadership was a two-horse race – Steel versus Pardoe. Inverness MP Russell Johnston failed to win sufficient backing from the parliamentary Liberal party to be nominated. In a flamboyantly gallant gesture, Pardoe had offered to propose Johnston if Steel would second him. But Steel knew that Johnston would take votes away from him rather than Pardoe and simply sat on his hands. Steel argued that for two candidates to join in nominating another would destroy the constitutional barrier to adequate nominations decided by the Manchester assembly. Emlyn Hooson also declared his intention of standing, but seeing he could not collect sufficient nominees, he withdrew and backed Steel.

As this was the first time an election organised in this way had been held by the Liberals – or indeed any British political party – no one really quite knew how to set about organising the campaign. Election strategists pointed out that it bore some resemblance to an American primary contest, but neither of the protagonists had the kind of funds to match the cash that American candidates spent in primary elections. Pardoe had a more formal campaign organisation headed by Lord Beaumont and with the weighty backing of Cyril Smith, while Steel's informal organisation was led by Clement Freud and Isle of Wight MP Stephen Ross in Parliament, with former Steel aide Archie Kirkwood and his current aide Andrew Gifford organising support in the country.

The Steel campaign team faced a tricky decision on election tactics. On most policies, both Steel and Pardoe had an identity of view. Only on the question of realignment politics was Steel slightly more definite than Pardoe, but the campaign team felt that this small difference could hardly be elevated into an election-winning issue.

So the campaign team, with Steel's backing, decided to differentiate between Steel's and Pardoe's political characters. The Steel strategists adopted a cold, calculating – even cruel – plan of campaign. They would depict Pardoe as a hot-headed zealot whose judgement was not always sound. Archie Kirkwood, Steel's former parliamentary aide, explains, 'We knew Pardoe would score with the party activists, because he would go into their meetings with bulging eyes and proclaim the gospel according to St John. We decided that Pardoe had to be given enough rope with which to hang himself.'

The Steel campaign managers reckoned that although Pardoe would go over big with the really keen party workers – those who give up night after night to canvass or deliver leaflets for the party – the ordinary member, the silent majority of Liberal voters, would be frightened off by Pardoe's aggression. So the campaign plan was for Steel to stress his calm, cool, clear and rational approach to politics, leaving Pardoe to his flamboyant and extravagant gestures. In the words of Archie Kirkwood, 'We felt that the mass of the membership would be more amenable to a quiet rational approach.' The only danger in this strategy was that Pardoe's supporters, who controlled most constituency associations, would activate the rank-and-file members to back their man. To overcome this danger, the Steel campaign managers reasoned that Pardoe had to be provoked into over-reacting.

It was while Steel was driving with Kirkwood and Gifford down the M90 to Edinburgh, after the 1976 Scottish Liberal party conference, that the three took a decision which set the leadership campaign alight. Pardoe had just stated in a newspaper interview that he was the most 'effective bastard' in politics. The three decided that if Pardoe was going to talk like this, it was time to send him up. That weekend Judy Steel came across an amusing passage in a book she was reading as a bedtime story for her children – The House at Pooh Corner. This described how Tigger got muddled up in a fight with a table cloth, and ended up poking his head out of the cloth and exclaiming, 'Have I won?'

The next day, Steel turned up at a rally of 600 Sussex Liberals in Hove Town Hall. Pardoe's fellow Cornishman, David Penhaligon, the MP for Truro, and the only MP with a genuine Cornish accent, delivered a laugh-a-line speech in support of his West Country champion. Steel, who had arrived late, stood at the back of the hall among the crowd and laughed as heartily as anyone else. Then his turn came to speak. He introduced the main themes of his campaign, and then produced his Pooh quotation, relating it to Pardoe's behaviour. The audience roared their approval, and it was clear that the shaft would strike home tellingly with Liberal members.

A few days later Steel, in a half humorous throw-away comment to two journalists, hinted that Pardoe wore a hairpiece. Pardoe, like many people who claim to be super-tough, is, in fact, extremely sensitive and was bitterly wounded by these taunts. He trumpeted about the 'drip, drip, drip of the total lie'.* Pardoe's keen supporter, Cyril Smith, weighed in with some vigorous attacks on Steel, who, he said, 'could not make a bang with a firework in both hands'. Smith also accused Steel of not supporting the new leadership election system. 'He is not in favour of this outbreak of democracy,' claimed Smith.

As the campaign drew to a close, it became obvious that Steel would win. He sought to cool the temperature of the campaign in a speech in Plymouth. 'I want to reaffirm there is no way in which I regard John Pardoe as an enemy,' he told his West Country audience. 'Do not be mislead by the teasing or verbal description of either of us. If John is elected, I shall serve loyally under him and do my best to take the party along the path he wants. If I am elected, I will regard his dynamism as indispensable to an effective team leadership.'

On 7 July, at the end of a long count in the Poplar Civic Theatre in East London, Steel was declared elected by a margin of 12,541 'national ' votes to 7,032 'national' votes. Altogether 69,726 party members had voted in the leadership election. A poll carried out by Marplan revealed that amongst the general public 64 per cent preferred Steel, compared with only 23 per cent who wanted Pardoe. Among Liberal voters, the margin had been wider, 68 per cent to 20 per cent.

* The saga of Pardoe's hairpiece had an amusing sequel. At a meeting of parliamentary Liberals about a year later, the subject of the leadership came up. Chief whip, Alan Beith, turned to Pardoe and said, 'John, was that true about your hairpiece?' The meeting went deadly silent, anticipating a Pardoe explosion. Ruefully, Pardoe admitted it was true, and the meeting dissolved into laughter.

On the stage of the Poplar Civic Theatre, Steel received messages of congratulation from the defeated Pardoe, and from temporary leader Grimond. There was even a message from Thorpe, who had cast his own vote for Steel. 'Now that the election is over, I ask every Liberal to give David their loyalty and enthusiasm,' he said, and added bitterly, 'I know he will need both.'

12

New directions

A revealing incident at London's Heathrow Airport a few days after Steel's election as Liberal leader perhaps indicated the kind of leader Steel planned to be. He was sitting quietly in the airport cafeteria drinking a glass of milk and eating a cheese sandwich. Although he had featured in the newspaper headlines for several weeks, nobody was taking any notice of him – except for one embarrassed airport official.

The official tentatively approached. 'Would Mr Steel be more comfortable in the VIP lounge?' he asked. The modest Steel thanked him, but assured the official he was quite comfortable where he was. 'But leading politicians always use the VIP lounge,' spluttered the official. 'I'm quite comfortable here,' Steel persisted. The official pressed Steel to repair to the VIP lounge. Again Steel refused. Finally, the tenacious official resolved the dispute by seizing Steel's milk and sandwich and carrying it off to the VIP lounge, Steel meekly following.

This incident sharply highlighted Steel's modest approach to his new position compared with that of his predecessor, Jeremy Thorpe. Few political leaders have been as unconcerned with the trappings of office as Steel. Yet few modern Liberal leaders have been as determined as Steel to seek political power for the party. In the months after his election to the leadership, Steel established a tight grip on the party and gave it a coherent new strategy. In the two years following the 1974 general elections, at which the Liberal party polled so well, there had been persistent rumblings about the lack of decisive leadership and direction. Admittedly, Thorpe had been fully occupied countering the threat posed to his position by the Scott affair. But Steel had already started to think in terms of a clear stragegy for the party based on the kind of realignment and coalition politics which he had espoused on entering politics.

His first task, however, was to establish his authority over the parliamentary Liberal party. The leadership election, in May, had opened up some sores in the party. Defeated John Pardoe was clearly upset by the result and some of Steel's campaign tactics. He muttered darkly about retreating to his Cornish heartland to work on his own political ideas. Even more troublesome, the emotional Cyril Smith, Pardoe's staunchest parliamentary backer, threw a public tantrum and threatened not to serve in a party post under Steel. He also announced he would not campaign in any constituency which had backed Steel in preference to his champion, which effectively ruled out most of the United Kingdom. Steel had to mollify both of these and weld together an effective parliamentary team under his leadership.

One of the big problems for any Liberal leader is to 'shadow' all government departments with just a handful of MPs. This normally means that each MP must take on a variety of jobs which would be shared around as many as six or seven people in the government or official opposition. It sometimes means that MPs have to cover subjects about which they have precious little knowledge and even less interest. Steel, however, coped with this problem well. A private discussion with Smith brought him back into the fold, and he accepted the spokesmanship on social services. The Truro MP David Penhaligon took over Smith's previous job as employment spokesman. Former leader Jeremy Thorpe accepted the foreign affairs portfolio — a natural choice in view of his high level diplomatic contacts abroad. Alan Beith stayed on as chief whip and became the party's education spokesman. The other Liberal MPs mostly retained their previous jobs with some minor alterations.

Steel's biggest problem clearly centred on what to do about Pardoe. Pardoe was the Liberal's foremost economic spokesman, and had built an enviable national reputation for the originality of his thinking. So it was natural that Steel should ask him to stay on in this post. Steel also wanted to use Pardoe's dynamism in the Liberal party's creaking organisation. Pardoe became Chairman of the party's influential Publications Committee. This Committee oversees the production of party pamphlets and leaflets, and therefore has a great influence on the way in which the Liberal message is presented to the public through Liberal literature. Steel had hoped to persuade the Liberals' National Executive Committee to abolish the separate Liberal News Board — which runs the party's weekly newspaper – and transfer the running of the paper to the Publications Committee. This would have given Pardoe the opportunity to co-ordinate all the party's propaganda media. But the idea never got off the ground, being stymied by the vested interests which often prevent sensible reform of the Liberals' organisation.

Election to the Liberal leadership meant some changes in Steel's life style. He moved into the small suite the Liberal leader occupies at the Commons, and he took charge of the party's small parliamentary research staff. But the new post also meant a financial sacrifice. Steel had been for several years a non-executive director of Hall Advertising Ltd, a leading Edinburgh-based agency. He had performed fairly nominal duties for this company, but the director's fees had been a useful supplement to the family income. Now, he felt, he had to relinquish the post. At the back of his mind was the embarrassment which Jeremy Thorpe had suffered as a result of the London and County Securities affair; he had been a director of the secondary bank which collapsed in unfortunate circumstances, although Thorpe had been absolved of any blame.

He also remembered Reginald Maudling's unhappy involvement with corrupt Yorkshire architect John Poulson. Steel had been especially outspoken about some aspects of the Poulson affair, and he believed that he should not risk comprising himself at all in commercial life.

Hall Advertising was – and is – a highly reputable and successful company, but Steel was concerned about any possible, unforeseeable conflict of interests. 'I feel that, unfortunately, the risks of being involved now in any kind of commercial activity are too great,' he says. 'That is a sacrifice which is now being demanded of politicians.'

With these preliminaries out of the way, and the summer recess upon him, Steel retreated to the calm of his Ettrick Bridge home to think out in more detail his approach to bringing the Liberal party to the centre of British politics. The Liberal assembly loomed in September, and in the traditional leader's address at the end of the assembly the party would expect Steel to point the way to a glowing future. Steel had no doubt in his own mind what that future should be. He was realistic enough to appreciate that the Liberals stand little chance of seizing power by themselves. There is, however, a real chance, Steel believes, that they could share in power with other parties, a theme he has coherently and consistently developed in speeches and articles throughout his eleven-year period in Parliament. Moreover, conditions were ripe for coalition talk. The narrow majority of Harold Wilson's Labour government was fast shrinking as a result of by-election losses. It was probable that before the lifetime of the Parliament was out, Labour would lose its overall majority.

A year earlier, Steel had attempted to spell out the Liberals' terms for a coalition, which would hinge on an 'early reform of the electoral system.' However, Steel made it clear this need not necessarily mean the introduction of a full-scale proportional representation voting system. The Liberals were prepared to discuss other approaches. Steel also pointed out that a national government would be useless if it gave way in two or three years to the old, class-bred, two-party system.

'It is no good the Tories hoping to form the next government, for, unless they believe in a one-party state, there has to be an alternative government after that. What is required is a long-term change which allows formation of new governments without the threat of a Marxist or an ultra-right-wing takeover.' Two months later, in July 1975, he gave another boost to the coalition cause. Although a coalition was not imminent, politicians should seriously consider it if the economic situation worsened, he said. 'We can be quite certain that the one thing which people don't want is to be plunged into another election. It would bring fresh impetus to our crisis and no conceivable result would solve anything.'

This talk annoyed hundreds of Liberal party workers. A meeting of the Liberal party Council – the Liberals' main policy-making body between annual assemblies – passed a resolution condemning any talk about 'Grand Coalitions'. This did not deter Steel from pressing ahead with his coalition campaign. On the same day the party Council was condemning his coalition talk, he was calling for a government which could rally a wide range of public opinion. 'If this government fails in the future to carry a parliamentary majority, then it must make way for one which will carry both parliamentary and public support. The experience of the referendum indicates that where a broad spectrum of politicians fight together for a purpose, they can rally public allegiance. The present government must, by its measures, appeal to the widest public and parliamentary loyalty. If it proves incapable of doing so, the duty of Parliament is to find one which will.'

Steel is not a man to change his views just because 'people disagree with him. And the fact that potentially thousands of Liberal members would tear up their party cards if he led the Liberals into a coalition did not deter him from his strategy. Many older Liberals remember with fear the Liberal involvement in coalitions in the 1920s and early '30s – coalitions which wrecked the electoral appeal of the party and split it into warring factions. They feared that any Liberal association with the other parties would invite history to repeat itself.

Steel does not hold this view. And during the long hot days of the 1976 summer, he put together a speech which was to be his political testament and point the Liberals towards an exciting new future. The by now famous Llandudno speech was largely Steel's own work. He worked out the pattern of the argument and the approach. But during that summer, his close advisers Richard Holme and William Wallace travelled to Ettrick Bridge to assist him. Steel likes to prepare his own speeches as far as possible, outlining the drift of his argument, but he welcomes the chance to talk over ideas with colleagues he trusts. In particular, he believes that Holme has the ability to supply the odd phrase which makes a speech flow better.

When Steel finally reached Llandudno in September with his speech in its final form, he found the party bitterly divided over talk of coalition politics. In particular, the Young Liberals, a perennial thorn in their elders' side, were furious that the party's integrity might be threatened by talk of coalition. As self-appointed custodians of the party's conscience, the Young Liberals opposed any move which might water down the purity of the faith.

Steel was himself concerned about the effect his speech might have. Rumours about its content had already reached delegates. In his suite at the Grand Hotel, Steel held urgent consultations about the text with other MPs and advisers. Some warned him that talk of coalition could produce a demonstration on the floor of the assembly. The Young Liberals threatened darkly about a floor demonstration if Steel even dared mention coalition in his address.

During these discussions, Steel had a long private meeting with John Pardoe, whom he had not seen since early summer. Pardoe had recovered from the bruising Steel gave him in the election contest. In the privacy of Steel's hotel suite, Pardoe said that as far as he was concerned the party had made its leadership choice. He would back Steel's leadership stragegy. This came as a great relief to Steel, for there had been suggestions that Pardoe might quit politics completely.

Despite the worries of colleagues, Steel decided that the party must confront the coalition issue. He explains, 'I thought it was necessary to deal with the coalition issue right away and not drift on in the way we had been doing. It really was necessary to do that, because the state of party morale was so low that something had to be done, if only to create a political argument again and get away from all the personality stuff in the wake of the Thorpe crisis.'

Steel rejected appeals to tone down his speech, although he came close to doing so. In the end, he rejected the views of his advisers and backed his own judgement. He says, 'I was afraid that if we didn't face the issue then, it was going to continue being a difficult and rumbling issue, as it had been since 1974. We'd had two years of irresolution on the whole issue and so I thought it better just to say what my views were.'

Steel adds, 'I did also feel quite strongly that my position was now stronger in leadership in relation to the rest of the party because I had been elected by the party at large, and therefore I could give a firmer direction than if I'd just been elected by the MPs.'

On the Saturday morning, the conference hall, brightly lit by television lights, was jammed with delegates. They had been carefully scrutinised on the way in by stewards for banners or other 'offensive weapons'. Steel stood in the wings and waited for his eleven o'clock cue when the television cameras would start broadcasting live from the assembly and he would walk on stage to a standing ovation.

He was shaking with nerves and his mouth had gone dry. He had taken a final decision the previous night. The passage on coalition would stay in the speech. What reaction this would provoke from the party, he could not say. There was even the chance the assembly could dissolve into chaos.

135

The clock ticked to eleven. Steel walked on stage to a rapturous standing ovation from the 2,000-strong audience. He stood at his lectern, poured himself a glass of water, took a deep breath and began. 'This has been an extraordinary year for Liberals ...' The 6,000-word speech, which had passed through countless drafts, is probably the most important Steel ever made. It had been skilfully constructed. Steel started by outlining in a humourous way how he had assumed the leadership of the party, and describing the abundance of advice he had received since doing so. 'I do not believe, however, that there is any one policy, one idea, one slogan which will ensure the success of the Liberal party, any more than I believe that any one man can achieve it. It's not as simple as that. And just as I want us to have a more collective leadership of persons, so I also want us to adopt clearly a set of attitudes which together add up to an appealing and cohesive vision of an alternative society.'

Steel built on this opening by describing the parlous state into which Britain had fallen. He argued that the two-party system had brought this about and added, 'We may not as people wish to end up as controlled digits in the Socialists' army, but neither do we intend to become sharp-toothed little predators in the Tory jungle.' He went on to discuss the poverty of Britain's political system, and the failure of successive governments to introduce proportional representation.

Steel argued that there were four policy priorities for Liberals. The first was to elevate the merits of frugality and thrift in the conduct of the nation's affairs. 'It is not growth of public expenditure which is wrong; it is the growth of wasteful public and private expenditure.' The second was to attack the growth of poverty. This meant changing the tax system, so that low-income earners would escape tax, and also reforming the social security system. The third priority was to reform the tax structure so that individual effort was rewarded. 'There is no longer any incentive for hard work, because both the high-paid executive and the modestly paid overtime-earning shop-floor workers can see little point in extra effort for the benefit largely of the Inland Revenue.' Finally, Steel urged the merits of the traditional Liberal policy of worker participation in industry.

He went on to suggest that the country could build more civilised communities if the virtues of self-help were rewarded.

'All that I am saying adds up to a plea for less government control, regulation and restraint. Why should we always look to government to solve problems when we can solve them ourselves? The "nanny" attitude to government has been encouraged by Tory and Labour administrations. We must change all this. Let us push back the frontiers of government.' Steel urged Liberals to fight against 'collectivism and statism'. 'Let the individual and group as far as possible be free to do its own thing. It is the most attractive way to live.'

Throughout this worthy but dull presentation of the Liberal case, Steel's audience remained tense, although they received his speech well. The speech had run for almost forty minutes – very nearly the full length of most leaders' addresses – and there was no talk of coalition. Indeed in one passage, Steel seemed to be moving away from coalition politics. 'There is no place for the Liberal party in the soft centre of political debate. We must be way out front. We must capture the new ground and high ground of politics,' he proclaimed. And he firmly stated that there was little chance of liberal values flourishing in the other political parties. 'Those who have preened themselves as repositories of wisdom and light in other parties have sold out to the system.' Both these statements raised loud cheers from the delegates.

Finally, Steel arrived at the nub of his argument. He visibly paused and took a sip of water. 'We must follow through the logical consequence of our own policies and utterances if we are to convince the public that we really mean business when we talk about being the only agent of hope and change.' The assembly went deadly silent, sensing the controversial statement to come. Impatient rustling of agenda papers abruptly ceased.

Steel ploughed on and was heard in complete silence. 'Let there be no misunderstanding. We are in being as a political party to form a government so as to introduce the policies for which we stand. That is our clear aim and object. But I, as leader, have a clear, obvious duty to assess how most speedily we can reach that objective. I do not expect to lead just a nice debating society.' The rustling started again as Young Liberals scattered throughout the hall reached into inside pockets and handbags for hastily written signs.

Steel spoke his next sentence clearly and slowly, pausing to take breath after every phrase. 'If we argue that we alone can be the means of transforming the sterility of British political life, if we tell the public that only by voting Liberal in sufficient numbers to prevent one other party gaining a majority will we achieve electoral reform and break the Tory/Labour stranglehold, then equally we must be clear in our own minds that if the political conditions are right (which of course they were not in February 1974) and if our own values are retained, we shall probably have – at least temporarily – to share power with somebody else to bring about the changes we seek.' Silently about fifty Young Liberals rose in their seats holding placards which read 'No Coalition' or just 'No'. The audience erupted into applause and angry delegates shouted at the Young Liberals to sit down. John Pardoe, next to Steel on the platform, was on his feet leading a one-man standing ovation.

Visibly shaken by the demonstration, Steel's voice rose perceptibly a pitch and he hurried on with his speech. 'Of course, neither of the other parties will want to relinquish their exclusive, alternating hold on power, but if the people won't let them have it, then they will have to lump it – Tory and Labour. I want the Liberal party to be the fulcrum and centre of the next election argument – not something peripheral to it. If that is to happen we must not give the impression of being afraid to soil our hands with the responsibilities of sharing power.

'We must be bold enough to deploy the coalition case positively. We must go all out to attack the other parties for wanting power exclusively to themselves no matter how small a percentage of public support. What I am saying is that I want the Liberals to be an altogether tougher and more determined force. I want us to be a crusading and campaigning movement, not an academic think-tank, nor minority influence, nor occasional safety valve in the political system.'

Then with a thrust at his opponents in the party, Steel concluded his argument. 'The road I intend to travel may be a bumpy one, and I recognise, therefore, the risk that in the course of it we may lose some passengers, but I don't mind, so long as we arrive at the end of it reasonably intact and ready to achieve our goals.'

In the furore and excitement of the speech, few people closely analysed what Steel actually said. His terms for power-sharing were so hedged about by clauses and sub-clauses that they allowed the Liberals to enter a coalition only under the most stringent conditions. However, the assembly speech had an important psychological effect on Steel. The rapturous reception he was given at the end of his speech − with a four-minute standing ovation − led him to believe he had won over the minds of the party. He had certainly captured the hearts of the Liberal activists in the hall at Llandudno, but their heads were still unsure about the whole concept of power-sharing. In the months that followed − critical months leading up to the Liberal agreement with the government − Steel believed that there was far wider support for coalition politics in the Liberal party than was actually the case. This gave him confidence to push ahead with the Lib-Lab pact when the opportunity came a few months later.

In fact, support in the Liberal party for pact politics was not nearly as widespread as the assembly ovation suggested, but Steel had clearly alerted the party to the kind of leadership he intended to provide.

13

The birth of the Lib-Lab pact

Although the Liberal party is ostensibly in business to form the government of the nation, at times it displays what amounts almost to an allergy to power. Close proximity to power tends to bring the party out in the political equivalent of a nasty rash which takes the form of agenda for Liberal meetings being spotted with dozens of resolutions giving all manner of reasons why the party should be wary of holding office. This is certainly an unusual reaction for a political party, especially when compared with its bigger brothers, the Conservative and Labour parties, which will do practically anything in order to obtain power.

This Liberal aversion to power has often puzzled political commentators. Many of them could not understand why, for example, Jeremy Thorpe rejected Ted Heath's overtures in March 1974, when there are scores of MPs in the other two parties who would sell their wives and children for a seat at the cabinet table. But many political commentators have failed to understand the Liberal party, because too often they have failed to understand the people who join the Liberal party. The average Liberal association consists of as agreeable a bunch of contradictory characters as you will find anywhere. Young Liberals, whose views make Marx seem like a member of the Primrose League, cheerfully rub shoulders with old ladies who would be delighted if Enoch Powell became Prime Minister. Between these two extremes it is possible to find Liberal members expressing virtually every shade of political opinion, for few Liberal members, let alone voters, really understand what the party's policies are. One example of this is the fact that opinion polls consistently show the majority of Liberal voters wanting Britain to quit the Common Market, even though the Liberal party has been the most consistently pro-European party.

It is, perhaps, not surprising that few people really know what the Liberal party's policies are. As the party has had no opportunity of implementing those policies in government for more than sixty years, they are somewhat academic. The result of this confusion is that every Liberal tends to have his own idea of what the ten most important Liberal policies are, and this applies to the parliamentary Liberal party as well as to ordinary Liberal members. About the only item which appears on every Liberal's list is proportional representation, and even here, although Liberals agree about the need for PR, they disagree about which system of PR should be used. It should be added that while the average voter feels that Britain's electoral system is unfair, he is so baffled by the technicalities of PR that, as an emotive vote-winning issue, the subject is an instant turn-off.

This short dissertation is germane to the whole way in which the Liberal party approached the Lib-Lab pact of 1977–8, and suggests why so little, in terms of implementation of specific policy proposals, was achieved.

Since the fall of the last Liberal government – that of Asquith in 1916 – Liberals have been in government on only four occasions this century. Lloyd George led a coalition consisting mostly of Conservatives from 1916 to 1922. In 1929 the Liberals, again led by Lloyd George, propped up a minority Labour government. In 1931 some Liberals participated in Ramsay MacDonald's National Government, while others opposed it. When Winston Churchill formed his wartime coalition in 1940, the leader of the Liberal party, Sir Archibald Sinclair, became Minister for Air.

None of these dalliances with power had a beneficial effect on Liberal electoral fortunes, and some Liberals maintain to this day that they contributed to the party's decline. So the omens for Steel's dream of Liberal influence over a Labour government were not good. But, then, Steel is no ordinary Liberal politician. On the face of it, no politician who wanted power would join a political party that has been out of power for sixty years. Steel wants power, yet that is precisely what he has done. But, unlike many other Liberal politicians, he has a clear idea of how he proposes to bring the Liberal party back into power. He knows exactly what he wants, and has the determination to get it. Thus, when in spring of 1977 the Liberals had the chance of co-operating with James Callaghan's faltering government, Steel was able to negotiate the pact, even though probably a majority of

Liberal members, and certainly a majority of Liberal voters, were against the idea. It is also probably true to say that no other Liberal leader since the war could have managed what Steel achieved in just four days of March 1977. He negotiated with his own sceptical party and a sceptical Prime Minister, and produced a parliamentary arrangement which substained the government in power for eighteen months.

Steel needed more than his clear idea of Liberal objectives to achieve this. He was greatly aided by the fact he had only recently been overwhelmingly elected leader of the party by the grass roots membership. During that leadership campaign, and immediately afterwards, he had made perfectly clear in which direction he intended to lead the party. He felt, therefore, that he had a mandate from Liberal members for the action he was taking. It is also true that Steel is thoroughly trusted by Liberal members, even though they do not always agree with his policies and tactics. He has an air of transparent honesty and integrity which disarms critics and gains respect from opponents. But allied to this, he has a degree of political cunning which sometimes seems almost essential to political success in Britain. During his negotiation of the pact, he was to manoeuvre his parliamentary colleagues as though they were chess pieces on a board, and virtually ignore the views of the Liberal party in the country at large. As he has often done in his political career, Steel displayed a single-minded determination to get what he wanted, despite the wishes of others.

A feature of governments in the last thirty years has been their propensity to lose by-elections heavily in the mid-term of a Parliament. Effectively, this means that any government which starts life with an overall majority of less than twenty must be a risky bet to end the Parliament five years later still firmly in power. Labour started with a majority of less than twenty.

That finally disappeared in 1976, when Labour lost previously safe seats in Workington and Walsall North. However, there was no immediate threat to Labour's position. With its devolution bills, which aimed to provide a measure of self-government to Scotland and Wales, still wending their tedious way through Parliament, the fourteen Scottish and Welsh Nationalists could be relied on not to bring the government down. However, devolution was bitterly opposed by a significant number of left-wing

Labour MPs. They finally scuppered the independence bill for Scotland and Wales in February 1977 by defeating a move to introduce a government guillotine in the committee stage of the bill.

After that, shorn of their dreams of Parliaments in Edinburgh and Cardiff, there was no reason why the Nationalists should keep Labour in power. Indeed, with Labour especially unpopular in these provinces, they reasonably assumed that an early election would bring a considerable increase in their parliamentary representation.

Meanwhile, Steel had been preparing the Liberal party for the inevitable moment when it would have to decide whether to keep the government in power or kick it out. After the success of his Llandudno speech – when he broached the subject of coalition – he assumed that the party was largely behind him. He followed up this speech with a controversial party political broadcast in November, when he spelt out to the nation at large why he believed the Liberals should seek power. This brought a storm of protest from Liberal purists, who wrote furious letters to *Liberal News*, complaining that the fragile flower of Liberalism was about to be defiled.

It was Britain's economic problems which finally put Labour on the spot. With inflation raging at more than 20 per cent, and the country in deep balance-of-trade difficulties, the hard-faced bankers of the International Monetary Fund ordered savage cuts in government spending as the price of bailing out Britain with a substantial loan. Chancellor Denis Healey had little choice but to obey, and in March 1977 he laid before the House of Commons plans to slash government spending by £2,500 million. The Conservatives, Liberals, Nationalists, Ulster Unionists and the tiny independent Scottish Labour Party announced they would all oppose this motion for a variety of reasons. Besides this, the government faced a sizeable revolt from the left wing of the Labour party from MPs who could not stand having their cherished socialist policies wrecked by international financiers. Government chief whip Michael Cocks predicted that Labour would lose the vote at the end of the parliamentary debate to ratify the measures. The opposition parties duly defeated the government, but the government showed no sign of wanting to resign, even though it could not obtain parliamentary approval for its spending policies.

The following day, a strident Margaret Thatcher, leader of the Opposition, announced she would table a motion of no confidence in the government which would be debated in the Commons the following Wednesday. If the government lost this vote, it would be out, and Jim Callaghan would be making the trip to the Palace to see the Queen.

During the next five days, political events started to move at an increasing pace. Following the critical vote on government cuts on Thursday night, Steel had quit the House of Commons and taken the night sleeper to Edinburgh. By Friday morning, while Mrs Thatcher was thumping the despatch box and threatening Armageddon on the scattering of hapless Labour Members on the benches, Steel was cheerfully going about his constituency business. He had scheduled a busy weekend of engagements starting with his regular 'surgery', where his constituents came to discuss their problems. Unlike many of his colleagues, who had started to cluck like nervous hens, he had his strategy quite clearly mapped out in his mind. Either the government would come to some kind of long-term arrangement with the Liberals in Parliament, or the Liberals would vote with the other opposition parties in the confidence debate and precipitate a general election. The prospect of an election did not especially worry him. He felt that the Liberals would do reasonably well in a campaign, and that by spelling out his clear realignment message during the election, the Liberals would return to Parliament with a parliamentary party not much changed from its present size.

Steel was sitting in his small constituency office, above a cafe in Galashiels' main street, when news of the Thatcher confidence motion reached him. While he was interviewing a constituent about some local problem, his agent Riddle Dumble popped his head round the door to say that Cledwyn Hughes, chairman of the parliamentary Labour party was on the phone. Steel had, in fact, had a friendly talk with Hughes just a few days earlier, when he had made it clear that the Liberals did not fear an election, but would be prepared to discuss some broadly based arrangement with the government. Hughes had duly reported back to the Prime Minister on this conversation.

What Hughes now told Steel on the telephone was that the expected Tory no confidence motion had been tabled. Steel broke off his surgery casework to issue an immediate statement via the Press Association.

It said, 'Either the government now proceeds on the basis of agreed measures in the national interest for the next two years, in which case we would be willing to consider supporting such a programme, or else we have a general election. The one thing we cannot do is stagger on like last night with a lame-duck Labour programme. The political decision as to which course to take therefore rests squarely with the Prime Minister and the Labour party.' Saturday's press mostly wrote off this statement as predictable Liberal sabre-rattling. With the Liberals down in the opinion polls, the pundits expected Liberal MPs to abstain meekly rather than risk their own seats.

Steel, in fact, strongly held the view that there was no particular advantage for the party in postponing the election for a few more months while Labour staggered on hopelessly. The following day, therefore, − Saturday − in a further press statement, he made his position abundantly clear. 'If the Labour party does not acknowledge the political reality that it cannot continue to push on with full-blooded socialist government, because there is no mandate for it, then the thirteen Liberal votes will be bound to be cast against the government in the confidence debate in favour of a general election, at which we would put our case for an end to the domination of Parliament by any one extreme − socialist or Thatcherite.' The statement said that Labour MPs would be 'committing suicide if they refused to compromise and seek a broader understanding in Parliament. It would be in the best interests of this country if it now begins to be governed on the basis of enjoying the widest possible public and parliamentary support for a programme of national recovery,' Steel added.

The tempo of events now increased even more. On Saturday afternoon, William Rodgers, the Transport Secretary, and a trusted member of Callaghan's cabinet, telephoned Steel at Ettrick Bridge. The call was in the nature of a fishing expedition to find what terms Steel would demand in the event of Callaghan considering some kind of pact. Rodgers, now a leading Social Democrat, was an excellent choice for this sounding-out exercise. Firstly, he had worked closely with Steel during the previous year's European referendum campaign and they had established a relationship of mutual rapport and trust. Secondly, Rodgers had spoken to *Guardian* guru Peter Jenkins, one of the most incisive minds in Fleet Street, earlier that afternoon. Jenkins had told Rodgers that at a private lunch with Steel a few days earlier, the Liberal leader had made it perfectly clear he had no intention of propping up the government without some definite formal arrangement.

Steel repeated his view to Rodgers that the government would have to offer some more broadly based agreement if it wanted the Liberal votes on Wednesday night. Rodgers then telephoned the Prime Minister, weekending at Chequers, to convey this message. That Saturday evening, his mind preoccupied with affairs of state, Steel went to watch his foster son, Billy, appear in a production of *My Fair Lady*. During the song-and-dance routines, Steel reflected that 'wouldn't it be luverly' if the Liberals could get a coalition agreement with the government.

On Sunday, Steel and his wife, Judy, had a luncheon engagement with their close friend John Mackintosh, then Labour MP for the neighbouring constituency of Berwick and East Lothian. But first he made a detour to Edinburgh to appear on ITV's *Weekend World* programme at midday. He was quizzed by interviewer Peter Jay – ironically, the Prime Minister's son-in-law – about the terms he would demand for entering a pact with the government. For Steel, it was a poor interview. At this delicate stage in the proceedings, it was not time to be making precise demands in television interviews. He waffled vaguely about government proceeding in the national interest and Labour dropping extreme left-wing measures, but added little concrete to his statements of the previous two days. After the interview and the lunch, the Steels returned to Ettrick Bridge. There he received more calls from Hughes and Rodgers, who said the Prime Minister would like to meet him early the following evening.

The invitation from Callaghan was important to Steel. He had always believed that it was essential for Liberal prestige that the initiative for talks should come from the government. Now that Callaghan had invited him to talk, Steel decided that he must win the full-hearted support of his colleagues for the tricky negotiations which were about to begin. So, that Sunday evening, Steel ensconsed himself in his cosy study and started calling his parliamentary colleagues in different parts of the country. To each his message was the same: the call had come from Callaghan; he must answer it to see what terms were on offer. None of the other Liberal MPs objected to Steel meeting Callaghan, although Jo Grimond and David Penhaligon expressed the strongest reservations.

Monday was a decisive day in pact politics. Steel had planned to start it by making a visit to boost the campaign of the Liberal candidate in the Birmingham Stetchford by-election. To fit in this by now somewhat unnecessary engagement, Steel drove rapidly to catch the 9.12 train from Carlisle to Birmingham. On the way, he ran over a pheasant. With true Scots canniness, he handed it to Judy to take back and cook. Cutting it fine for the train, Steel put his foot down. As he roared into Carlisle a policeman stopped him. When the officer saw whom he had stopped, he kindly waved Steel on. 'I know you're rushing to see the Prime Minister,' he said.

The Stetchford visit over, Steel proceeded to London for his meeting with Callaghan. In a preliminary wrangle with the Prime Minister's office, Steel had ruled out the prospect of Deputy Prime Minister Michael Foot attending the meeting. If Foot was to be present, John Pardoe, his own deputy should go, too, Steel said. Shortly after six o'clock, Steel strolled round to the Prime Minister's suite in the House of Commons and the hard negotiating began.

In Steel's mind, the meeting had two purposes. The first was to establish whether there actually was the basis for some kind of arrangement. The second was to build some kind of rapport with Callaghan. Steel had only briefly met Callaghan before, and hardly knew him personally. He felt strongly that the success of any pact would depend on a bond of trust between the leaders of the two parties which entered it.

Callaghan greeted Steel in his usual cordial avuncular manner. He waved Steel to a seat beside him, and plunged straight into the business in hand. Callaghan asked Steel what the Liberals' voting intentions were for the Wednesday-night confidence vote. He said that if the government lost the vote there would be a general election in which, he felt, both the Labour and Liberal parties could do badly. Was there any basis on which the Liberals would agree to support the government in Wednesday's vote?

Steel was not surprised that Callaghan still wanted to discuss

147

Liberal co-operation in terms of getting through Wednesday night's vote, even though he had already made it clear to both Hughes and Rodgers that the Liberals would require some more broadly based agreement. Steel told Callaghan politely but bluntly that if all the government wanted was some kind of covert deal to get them through Wednesday's vote, then the two parties had no basis for discussion. Steel says, 'Callaghan accepted this point quickly. In fact, I was surprised how quickly he accepted it.' Steel and Callaghan talked for just over an hour. At the end of the discussion, Steel left with enough encouragement to feel a deal might be on.

Despite this, he instructed the Liberal party Chairman Geoffrey Tordoff and Secretary General Hugh Jones to prepare for a general election. This was basically a window-dressing exercise and fulfilled two needs – to keep the press guessing which way the Liberals would jump, and to convince sceptical Labour MPs that the Liberals would opt for a election unless the terms were right.

Later on Monday night, Steel called a crucial meeting of his parliamentary colleagues. At 10.45 the thirteen Liberal MPs squeezed into Steel's room at the House. Steel outlined the progress which had been made so far in the talks with the Prime Minister, and asked their permission to proceed further. There was a general air of excitement about the meeting. Everyone was trying to talk at once, and Steel had difficulty in keeping control of the meeting. He told the MPs that a report compiled by the party organisation showed that the party was reasonably prepared for a general election. As a result of this, the party should feel no compulsion to enter a pact. But he told them that here was a real chance for the party to experiment with the realignment politics which it had been preaching for twenty years. For just over an hour the meeting lurched around the subject, but although most MPs expressed their ideas about what the party should seek to obtain from a pact, there was no attempt to draw up a formal list of demands to put to Callaghan. Significantly, this was left to Steel.

The following morning, he sat down at his desk and scrawled out in his semi-legible handwriting the Liberals' initial bid. The document contained six main points. First, a consultative committee was to be set up between the government and the

Liberal party to review government business. Secondly, there was to be an immediate meeting between Chancellor Denis Healey and Liberal economics spokesman John Pardoe 'to confirm that there is sufficient identity of view on our economic strategy'. Thirdly, the government was to introduce and commend to the House a bill for direct elections to the European Parliament. Fourthly, the government was to resubmit its legislation on devolution for Scotland and Wales. Fifthly, there was to be no more nationalisation, and the Local Government Direct Labour Bill was to be dropped. Finally, the terms of any agreement had to be published in an exchange of letters.

Subsequent critics have suggested that this was an amazingly thin list of demands, considering that the Liberals were throwing a lifeline to a drowning government. To understand their significance fully, one has to appreciate the position Steel found himself in and the pressures which were being applied. By now, Steel was himself sold on the idea of some kind of arrangement with the government. Throughout his whole political life, he had argued for some form of power-sharing as a way back to political relevance for the Liberal party. Now at last, a combination of political circumstances presented themselves which could not be relied on to occur again for twenty-five years or more. Steel was determined that he would not pitch his demands so high that Callaghan would be obliged to turn them down. For Steel, the key point in the agreement was the consultative committee. Through this committee, the Liberal party could be seen by the whole nation to be sharing in the business of government. Moreover, the existence of the committee, Steel reasoned, would help to scotch the notion in the public mind that only one-party government could work effectively.

In this context, the actual policy demands – including the demand for direct elections to the European Parliament – were of subsidiary importance to Steel. In any event, he reasoned, if the pact worked, it would be a developing animal, and there would be a whole range of future issues upon which the Liberals could exercise influence. The pact did not commit Liberals to vote with the government on every issue, only on motions of confidence when the government's survival was at stake. Hence, once the pact was under way, the Liberals could up the stakes and demand more concessions from the government as issues arose. In this light, the original list of demands – essentially a first bid to get the game under way – was of much lesser importance than contemporary commentators suggested.

At the same time, the first bid did have to satisfy the sceptical Liberals who would want to be assured they were getting something positive out of the arrangement. Hence, the importance of direct elections by proportional representation to the European Parliament. This issue, of no importance to the mass of the British people, assumed an air of totem-like significance to Liberals. They felt that if proportional representation was used for just one election in Britain, it would surely in time creep into others. Most of the detailed discussions on the terms were to centre on the Liberal demands for direct elections, not so much because Steel regarded this issue of overriding importance – he did not – but because he knew that unless he could deliver a reasonable deal on this one item, the whole pact was likely to founder in the face of his colleagues' and the party's hostility.

The demands in Steel's letter landed on the Prime Minister's desk shortly after eleven o'clock on Tuesday morning. An hour and a half later, Steel strolled round for another meeting with Callaghan. At this meeting, Callaghan was accompanied by Michael Foot, and advisers Ken Stowe and Tom McNally. Steel left the meeting after a brief thirty-minute chat with the distinct impression that his six points would be well received. Early that afternoon, he reported back to his colleagues. Since the previous evening, their determination on the question of PR for the European elections had stiffened. They insisted that the government commit itself to legislate for this, or else no deal.

Steel shuttled back to the Prime Minister with his fresh information later that afternoon. Callaghan showed Steel a copy of a White Paper the government proposed to publish on direct elections. This described two systems – the first-past-the-post voting system and a proportional representation scheme – but the White Paper did not state which the government preferred. Steel said that his colleagues regarded it as a matter of prime importance that the government should express a definite preference for proportional representation. But Callaghan, aware of hostile pressures in his own party, was unwilling to go this far. He explained that he could not promise something that other MPs would not support, but gave a private assurance that he himself would vote for PR.

At 6.30, Steel summoned his parliamentary colleagues again to his office and read the riot act to them. The crunch had now come, he said. Either they must decide that they wanted a pact, in which case they must accept the principle of it, or they must face an inevitable general election. What they could not do, he bluntly told them, was go on arguing about points of detail like proportional representation for direct elections. Steel also reminded his colleagues of the important point that they would not be committed to vote with the government on every issue. Faced with this ultimatum from their new leader, the parliamentary Liberal party agreed to a pact, providing the final details could be concluded to their leader's satisfaction.

When Steel had his final meeting with Callaghan at about ten o'clock that night, he had virtually a free hand to commit the party to a pact. Pardoe, who accompanied Steel to the meeting, started by raising some awkward points with Callaghan, and for a time it seemed that the final discussion might founder on points of detail. But then Pardoe left for a prearranged television interview on the *Tonight* programme, and Steel was left alone to stitch up the deal. Around midnight, he phoned his colleagues to say the deal was on. Thus, the pact was agreed subject to cabinet approval. There had been no formal discussion in the parliamentary party about the final terms on offer, no vote on those terms, still less any consultation with the Liberal party in the country. The pact was undoubtedly Steel's baby. Once again, he had got what he wanted.

The next day, Steel in the third speech of the no-confidence debate spelt out the advantages of the pact as he saw them. He did so against a hubbub of furious Tories, who had seen the prospect of a famous parliamentary victory followed by a stunning Conservative win at the polls snatched from them.

Within twelve years of becoming an MP and only eighteen months after ascending to the leadership of the Liberal party, Steel had achieved his political objective – Liberal influence over the government of the day. Moreover, he had wheedled a sceptical Prime Minister and an unwilling parliamentary party into an arrangement which was to determine the style of government in Britain for one and a half years. When, in the months to come, critics were to complain about the lack of the pact's successes, they might have been reminded of Samuel Johnson's comment on female preachers: 'Like a dog walking on his hind legs – it is not done well, but you are surprised to find it done at all.'

14

Life under a Lib-Lab government

The Lib-Lab pact was forged in the fire of a Commons confidence vote in March 1977. It ended, not with a bang but with a whimper, in the early autumn of 1978. Thus, for eighteen months, the government of Britain relied on 'the active co-operation of two political parties, a unique political experiment in postwar Britain.

Steel has himself chronicled the events of the pact − or agreement, as he prefers to call it − in a published diary, an agreeable blend of shrewd political insights and sub-Crossman style gossip (*A House Divided*, Weidenfeld and Nicolson, London, 1980).

The brief history of the Lib-Lab pact was, for Steel, dominated by three main objectives − welding his colleagues into an effective shadow administration, keeping the pact alive in the Liberal party, and selling the pact in the country as a living example of coalition politics. Opinions vary on how successful Steel was in achieving these objectives, but a fair marking might be B minus for the first objective, B plus for the second and C for the third. This is not to underestimate Steel's achievement, for the pact was a unique constitutional arrangement conducted under acutely difficult political circumstances.

Not the least of these difficult circumstances was getting the Liberal party, both in Parliament and the country, to accept the realities of the situation. Throughout the full eighteen-month period there were incessant demands from some Liberals to end the arrangement, demands which tended to receive a disproportionate level of publicity from a hostile press. In the long run, the Liberal party lost very few active members, and may even have gained some. In the short term, the effects of the pact were fairly disastrous on Liberal electoral fortunes. Just two months after the pact had been concluded, the Liberals lost three-quarters of their county councillors in local elections throughout

Britain. In only two by-elections during the period did the Liberal vote hold up reasonably well – at Saffron Walden and Penistone.

As a result of the nervousness in his party, Steel had to take the pact in stages, the first up to the summer recess in 1977, the second to the Liberal special assembly in January 1978, the third up to the budget of 1978, and the fourth and final stage up to the end of the 1978 parliamentary session, effectively in the summer of that year. During these stages, he needed to muster his full authority as party leader to keep the pact on the rails. In fact, there were times when the pact seemed to be not so much between the Liberal and Labour parties as between David Steel and James Callaghan.

Steel had decided from the start that the success of the pact would largely depend on building a bond of mutual confidence. And he had a notable success in winning Callaghan's confidence to the extent that Callaghan would occasionally favour Steel with embarrassing items of confidential information about important security or other matters. Both Steel and Callaghan soon found that they had something in common – they enjoyed the exercise of power, and the cut and thrust of politics. However, neither was under the illusion that the partnership was one of equals.

Many of the problems which Steel had in selling the pact to his party and to the country at large, derived from this self-evident fact. Labour had 310 MPs in the House, the Liberals just 13, something like a thirty-to-one ratio. Moreover, the government was backed by the full power of the civil service, whereas the Liberals had to rely for background support and research on the resources of an underfinanced party. As a result of this, the effect of the pact was to be more negative than positive – stopping unpopular left-wing measures such as more nationalisation or the extension of trade union power. There was some value in this, as Steel saw it, because it provided a more stable climate in which business could operate. During the period of the pact the economy improved notably, with inflation and interest rates falling and output rising.

But of specific Liberal measures, there were few. The most notable was a tentative move towards profit-sharing, a long-cherished Liberal objective, in the 1978 Finance Bill. The Liberals failed to obtain proportional representation for the European elections, perhaps their most desired aim, but this was never a realistic prospect. On Scottish and Welsh devolution, the Liberals managed to achieve a positive input into the government's plans, but this was too little and too late to get a wholehearted commitment from a suspicious Labour party to the kind of far-reaching devolution proposals the Liberals wanted. On too many of these issues, Steel had to intervene personally to get an agreement with the government. The machinery of the pact — the bipartisan meetings between ministers and Liberal spokesmen, and the consultative committee — worked with only patchy success, and whenever difficulties arose they tended to be referred to Steel for a decision. This placed an intolerable burden on him, and reduced the time and energy he could expend on selling the pact to the party and to the country.

Steel succeeded in keeping the pact on the rails for eighteen months, despite the hostility or suspicion of a significant section of the party. In votes on the pact at Liberal assemblies, opponents never mustered more than a third of the delegates, but this was enough to mean that Steel had to devote a substantial portion of his time to arguing the case for his policy within the party. The most difficult period came before the special assembly in January 1978, when he threatened to resign if the party failed to follow his policy.

Steel had far less success in selling the pact in the country at large. With hindsight, he frankly admits that he underestimated the extent and depth of hostility towards the pact displayed by the Tory party and the Tory press. The issue was clouded because the Tories presented the pact as a cynical device to save Liberal skins from an election in which they would be bound to do badly. In fact, Steel would have been quite happy to have an election in March 1977. He believed — and he is probably right in this judgement — that the Liberal party would have done reasonably well in an election held at that time. But the Tory lie stuck, and clouded the public's view of Liberal motives for entering the pact. In any case, the argument for coalition politics is a subtle one. It takes time to explain, especially to a public used to seeing political issues presented in the media in stark black-and-white terms. Because many newspapers were hostile to the pact, they gave more space to Liberals who were opposed to the pact than to those who wanted to argue in its favour. Thus, the occasions when Steel could deploy the case fully were strictly limited. And there were hiccups in the pact which the press gleefully exploited.

The first hiccup came shortly after the pact had been signed, sealed and delivered over the joint signatures of Steel and Callaghan. Although Liberal economics spokesman John Pardoe had had an early meeting with Chancellor Denis Healey, it was too late to affect the shape of the 1977 budget. In that budget, Healey proposed to raise petrol tax by five and a half pence. This move greatly upset the Liberal MPs, who have mostly rural constituencies, where a car is essential, and where, in any event, petrol costs more than in urban areas. However, because they were committed to support the government, the Liberal MPs were obliged to vote for the budget resolutions which the government needed to pass in order to be able to start collecting the increased revenue. Afterwards, Liberal MPs hinted that they would seek to amend the Finance Bill, which would give the content of the budget legislative effect, so that the petrol tax increases were trimmed back. In a typically rumbustious speech during the budget debate, Pardoe seemed to suggest that the Liberals would vote against the tax increase. The following morning, the press carried reports suggesting the government would be defeated when the Liberals voted against the increases. The government was furious.

Over the next two days Pardoe held meetings with Treasury ministers on the subject, but they did not get anywhere. The government was insistent that the increases had to go ahead. More ominously, Callaghan weighed into the argument to make it plain that it was vital the budget resolutions should be passed. Passage of the resolutions was essential for the government to continue to collect its revenue, and Callaghan said that their passage would be regarded as an issue of confidence in the government. The Treasury Finance Secretary revealed this in a meeting with Pardoe.

Pardoe immediately telephoned Steel, who was on a weekend morale-boosting tour of Lancashire. For Steel, the problem was more than a small teething difficulty. It affected the viability of his whole new infant – the Lib-Lab pact. That afternoon he telephoned his office and arranged a meeting with Callaghan for the following Monday. Then he dictated a press statement which left no doubt that the Liberals would vote with the government on the petrol tax increases. He completed his Lancashire tour and then repaired home to Ettrick Bridge for the weekend. During late Saturday and Sunday, he telephoned one by one his colleagues around the country to win their approval for the action he had taken. It was not the first time Steel had sought retrospective approval for action he had already taken, nor was it to be the last. By the time he strode into Callaghan's office in the Commons on Monday morning, all but two of his colleagues – Geraint Howells and Clement Freud – had agreed. At a subsequent meeting of the parliamentary Liberal party, Steel read the riot act. Leaks to the press would have to stop, he told his stunned colleagues. The government would not want to deal with a 'bucket shop'.

Time and again, throughout the life of the pact, Steel had to step in personally to resolve issues which the other Liberal MPs were not able to finalise with the government. Often these were issues of quite minor importance. One was the election of directors to the Post Office Board. The government had proposed that worker directors, appointed by the Post Office unions, should sit on the Board of the Post Office. This was opposed by the Liberals. They wanted worker directors – but they wanted them elected directly by employees, not appointed by unions. The Liberals also wanted a consumer voice on the Post Office Board. The issue rumbled on through several meetings of the consultative committee. It was not until the end of April, when Steel personally intervened in the disputes, that the question was resolved with a compromise plan whereby the number of seats on the Board was increased to provide a larger consumer voice.

As the spring and early summer months of 1977 wore on, Steel turned his mind to getting the pact renewed in the autumn. This involved carrying the parliamentary party with him, and heading off some expected hostility at the party assembly in Brighton that September. Steel did not want the assembly to debate the terms on which the pact would be renewed. He rightly suspected that the party assembly would try to impose a long shopping list of demands for the continuation of the pact. Unlike many other Liberals, Steel recognised that it was pointless asking for things which the government could not deliver.

In any event, as June approached, Steel personally doubted whether the pact could continue, because the Labour party found it hard to come together on controversial issues. This came to a head in the committee stage of the Finance Bill, when Labour left-wingers combined with the Tories to pass popular tax-cutting amendments. Liberal representative John Pardoe was left supporting the official government line, much to his deep chagrin. On 14 June, Steel took to the air in a party political broadcast to spell out the future of pact politics. He delivered a clear warning that the future of the pact could be jeopardised if Labour MPs did not regularly line up behind their own government's policies. He told his audience, 'I am not sure whether we will be able to secure another agreement, because the Labour party is proving a difficult, fragile and internally divided partner. Unless they pull themselves together, we may have to have an election in the autumn. But I am sure we are right to try this new experiment in political co-operation. For the first time since the last war, politicians are sinking their differences to try to solve the country's problems. We may not succeed, but surely it is worth trying.' The broadcast was generally well received for its blunt, honest approach.

John Pardoe was also worried about the future of the government's pay policy. The first two stages of the policy had considerable success in bringing down the inflation rate from a near-disastrous 30 per cent. But with unions making truculent noises, there were serious doubts about whether phase three of the pay policy, due to start in the autumn, would be sufficiently effective to continue reducing the rate of inflation. Pardoe has always had an almost paranoic concern with inflation, regarding it as one of the modern evils of society. He has successfully convinced Steel of this view.

To consider that and other problems, Steel assembled his parliamentary party at the St Ermins Hotel, Westminster, for the weekend of 26 and 27 June. The purpose: to decide the terms upon which the Liberals would renew their pact with the government. In some of the MPs' minds there was even the heretical thought that the pact should not be renewed. Not in Steel's. He had so far enjoyed his taste of power and was determined that the pact should continue.

However, Steel did not get all his own way. He would have liked a simple arrangement with the government whereby the Liberals concentrated on obtaining a few really solid advances in key areas. Instead, each Liberal MP had his own ideas about what he wanted. It was like a mini-version of a Liberal assembly, where dozens of worthy motions demanding the immediate implementation of schemes varying from a barrage across the river Severn to a free legal service are passed by acclamation. The MPs produced a list of more than forty policy objectives. In the end, they narrowed their list down to ten key points:

1 Tax reform and income tax cuts
2 Profit-sharing for employees in industry – a hallowed Liberal policy
3 More incentives for small businesses and the self-employed
4 Reform of the Official Secrets Act – a Clement Freud hobbyhorse
5 Help for first-time home-buyers
6 A national efficiency audit – a grand but vague Pardoe-Wainwright programme
7 A youth employment scheme
8 Reform of the Monopolies Commission to improve consumer protection
9 Progress on devolution with Assemblies for Scotland and Wales elected by proportional representation
10 Direct elections to the European Parliament by proportional representation.

The list had its strengths and weaknesses. Its strong point was that it did contain something for everyone. Its weak point was that most of the objectives were framed in such a vague way that the government could appear to make concessions on them – for instance, by publishing a consultative document – without actually achieving any practical progress.

When the meeting broke up on Monday afternoon, Steel immediately walked round to Downing Street for a meeting with the Prime Minister. They met in Callaghan's study. Both men were in an affable and relaxed mood, Steel because he had got his colleagues to back the pact for another year, Callaghan because he reckoned that it would mean there was no need to call an election for several months yet. Callaghan told Steel that the ten points were acceptable in principle.

However, the pact renewal was not yet officially agreed. With potential union truculence over another stage to the government's incomes policy, there was a distinct risk that escalating wage demands could send the inflation rate spiralling upwards again. Steel was under considerable pressure from economics spokesman John Pardoe to insist on the continuing fight against inflation as a prerequisite of continuation of the pact. On 18 July, the parliamentary party met to review the prospect of renewing the pact. Several members were acutely unhappy about the prospect – notably Jo Grimond and Cyril Smith – but Steel carried the majority with him for renewal. The following week Steel had another meeting with Callaghan to finalise a draft agreement which could be put to their respective colleagues. By 25 July, Steel had badgered the doubters in the parliamentary party into accepting another session of pact politics. A statement announcing the renewal said, 'On 23 March the parliamentary Liberal party agreed to work with the government for the remainder of the parliamentary session in the pursuit of economic recovery. Having reviewed the operation of the agreement we have decided to continue co-operation into the next session of Parliament for so long as the objectives set out in the Chancellor's statement of 15 July [which dealt with the fight against inflation] are sustained by the government. We are agreed that the fight against inflation and unemployment is of paramount national importance, and stress the need for both the twelve-month gap between pay increases and the limit on the general level of earnings increase to 10 per cent.' This statement included a sensible release clause in case the economy started to go wrong.

With the pact renewed before the end of the parliamentary session, Steel returned to his constituency for the recess with a certain satisfaction. With the policy assured, he could concentrate on selling it to the Liberal activists who gathered for the Liberal party assembly in Brighton in September. Normally, the leader of the party waits until the final day of an assembly before addressing the adulating multitude, but Steel saw distinct risks in this. He had to set the tempo of the assembly. He had to tell them what he felt about the pact before they started passing all sorts of weird and wonderful resolutions about it.

So, immediately after the ceremonial preliminaries were over in Brighton's Dome Theatre, Steel rose to give a sergeant-majorly report to his troops. His speech, although not widely acclaimed, is in fact one of the best he has ever made. It was entirely right, Steel said, that the assembly should assess the effect of the pact, and he continued, 'First, there is no doubt that we have lost some public support. Part of this was foreseeable and in my view inevitable in the short run. One of the Tory commentators wrote, "The electors who built up the Liberal vote for years have been the electors who have used the Liberal party as their outlet for protest when angry with the Conservatives." He is possibly quite right. But frankly, I have never thought that there could be a secure or expandable future for the Liberal party as a kind of convenient temporary wastepaper basket for the ballot papers of discontented Tories. (*Wild cheering*)

'As to party activists, we have lost scarcely any parliamentary candidates or national or local officers. But we have lost some members, though gaining others. I said last year that the road I intended to travel would be a bumpy one and that we might therefore lose some of the passengers.' Then, in an uncharacteristically bitter thrust, he added, 'Some of them must have had a pretty tenuous hold on the vehicle, for they fell off at the first pot-hole.'

Steel also invoked the ghost of Lloyd George to answer those who said the pact should be broken off if certain policies were not agreed. In 1931, Lloyd George had told the Liberals keeping Ramsay MacDonald's minority government in power, 'We are in the position of a body of men whose sole sanction to enforce their behests is capital punishment. There are two objections to that. You cannot inflict capital punishment for minor offences, and you can only inflict it once for any offence.' Steel addressed the assembly again at its close. The delegates cheered as loudly as ever, and Steel journeyed back to Ettrick Bridge convinced that the bulk of his party was still loyally behind him in the pursuit of pact politics.

The assembly had rejected a resolution for the renegotiation of the pact by 716 votes to 385, but ominously, the assembly had passed an amendment to the resolution demanding that Labour MPs support proportional representation for Europe by 'a substantial majority' as the price for Liberals' continued support of the pact. For many Liberals, this issue was a sticking point, a test of Labour commitment to pact politics. As a result of long negotiations with the government, Steel and his colleagues had persuaded Callaghan to include proportional representation in the body of the Bill which the government had drafted to set up the machinery for direct elections to the European Parliament. The government adopted an unusual device of having a fall-back

161

clause included as an appendix to the Bill. This provided for using the first-past-the-post system of voting in single-Member constituencies.

When Parliament reassembled in the autumn, the Bill ground steadily towards the big vote. Callaghan announced to the parliamentary Labour party that he would personally vote for the Bill, and commended it to his colleagues, but although asked by Steel, he refused to order a whipped vote of all Labour Members. When the vote took place on 13 December, PR was defeated by 87 votes, largely because of an unofficial three-line whip against the principle of proportional representation by the Tories. A bare majority of Labour MPs supported PR.

After the debate, the Liberal MPs in a bitter and angry mood gathered in Steel's office to discuss the implications of the vote. There were calls to break the pact there and then. Finally, Steel walked round to Callaghan's room. Callaghan told Steel that a majority of Labour Members had supported PR, and asked what the Liberals would do now, Steel said that he did not know, but the parliamentary Liberal party would meet next day to discuss the situation.

He returned to his office and bluntly told his colleagues, 'He's going to see the Queen tomorrow.' There was a stunned silence, and by some accounts, some Members felt physically sick. But Steel had made his point. He wanted his colleagues to see what the prospect of fighting a general election on the issue of PR for Europe would be like.

December 14, 1977, was a bleak day in Steel's political life. He could see his cherished Lib-Lab pact crashing around him, and some fancy footwork was needed to hold his parliamentary party together. After a sleepless night, Steel was not in peak form to chair a meeting of the parliamentary party. They moaned and complained about the position, but deferred any action until after Steel had met the Prime Minister later that day. Steel pointed out to his restless colleagues that the government had stuck to the letter of the agreement made the previous July – the government had commended proportional representation to the House. If the Liberals were now to end the pact, Steel argued, it would be the Liberals who had broken it, not Labour. That afternoon Steel had a further meeting with Callaghan, but neither could add much to what they had told each other the previous evening.

By now, a head of steam was building up in the parliamentary party to end the pact. Liberal MPs such as John Pardoe and Cyril Smith had taken to the air to denounce in savage tones the Labour MPs who voted against proportional representation. From Liberals in the country, calls to end the pact were already pouring into the House by phone and telegram. When he faced his parliamentary colleagues at six o'clock that evening, in committee room J of the House, Steel knew that once again he had a stern fight to save the pact, which was so much his personal creation.

He opened the meeting by telling his colleagues again that the Liberal party could not in all conscience break the pact. Then he said that the argument in the Liberal party at large had to be resolved. The special assembly which the Liberal party Council had demanded must be held, and the Liberal MPs should attend and fight for the continuation of the pact. After an hour and a half of bitter argument, Steel sounded out the opinion round the table. Six wanted the pact to continue, four wanted it to end, and two abstained; one was absent. Steel had scraped through by the skin of his teeth.

The situation which had now arisen was the most serious challenge yet to Steel's political career, and it had arisen because most Liberal party workers' adherence to the ideal of pact politics was only skin-deep. If the special assembly rejected the continuation of the pact, they would be in direct conflict with their leader's strategy for leading the party. Although the assembly could not technically force its will on the parliamentary party, for the Liberal MPs to adopt a diametrically opposed policy would bring them into a position of such bitter conflict that the parliamentarians' position would become untenable. The party would be, perhaps irreparably, split. In short, Steel would either have to change his strategy or his position would become impossible and he would have to resign.

The day after the important meeting and yet another sleepless night, Steel sat down at his desk in the Commons and started his campaign to regain the heart of the party he led. He penned a blunt letter which was sent to Liberal candidates throughout the country. In it he told them, 'I think the party would be crazy to change course, but you are entitled to do so if you wish at the special assembly.' Speaking for himself, he told them, 'I am not going to change course now.' Steel outlined the history of the agreement and his view that Labour had adhered to the strict terms of the agreement.

Then he added, 'A small group of thirteen, especially if divided among themselves, cannot go against the decision of our assembly on its entire strategy and keep the Liberal party intact. Therefore, if you decide to break off the agreement, it will be broken. I could not be party to breaking the agreement delivered over my signature to the Prime Minister. Nor could I lead the party into an election arguing a case in which I do not believe. No party can put its leader in that position.' Steel was using the oldest ploy in the political book – the threat to resign. It worked.

When the special assembly met in Blackpool in January, Steel led the debate in favour of continuing the pact from the floor of the conference hall. There was much grumbling, but he won the day by a massive 1,200 votes, one of the largest margins ever in a controversial debate at a Liberal assembly.

Nevertheless, the parliamentary defeat of proportional representation for Europe and the mood of the special assembly effectively killed any lingering hope that Steel had entertained of carrying the pact on into a third session of Parliament in the autumn of 1978. The terms needed by Steel in order to satisfy his party would be so demanding that Callaghan could not grant them. In any event, by the time the summer came, Pardoe was warning that the economy could worsen during the coming winter – as, in fact, it did – and that it would be unwise for the Liberal party to be associated with the government during this period.

The remaining months of the pact brought only a few concessions, the main one being a cautious move, contained in the Finance Bill, towards Liberal-style profit-sharing schemes in industry. Steel finally announced that the pact would not be further renewed on 25 May, although he continued to remain in contact with Callaghan until September. In September Callaghan, to Steel's deepening chagrin, announced that he planned to continue the government through to the next year, 1979. Steel said, 'The country had expected an election and will be disappointed. The sooner the government goes to the country the better. We shall act accordingly.'

Steel views the pact as having been a limited success. In his opinion, it helped to control inflation, it provided essential parliamentary stability, it showed that bipartisan government works, and it made some progress towards his cherished profit-sharing policy. He is fond of comparing the economic record of the Lib-Lab pact period, with its falling inflation and mortgage rates, with the economic record of the Thatcher government. It is true that not many specifically Liberal policies were implemented during the period, but Steel does not regard this as being a key factor in evaluating the pact's success.

Far more important is the fact that the Liberals, for the first time since the war, had a taste of power. From being an irrelevance on the fringe of politics, they suddenly became central to the determination of policy. From thinking about their own policies in vague, woolly and idealistic ways, they suddenly had to tailor their ideas to the exigencies of power. All this had provided a salutary lesson for the Liberal party, and given it a much more purposeful role in politics.

Moreover, as a speech on coalition politics made by Steel in the summer of 1978 showed (see chapter 15), he had also learnt some key lessons about the tactics and practice of coalition politics in Britain. Few other British politicians have given as much detailed and practical thought to this subject as Steel has. In a Britain in which two out of the three last governments have not had an overall parliamentary majority this is a serious omission in political thinking. If another election should produce a hung parliament – and the emergence of a Liberal–Social Democrat alliance makes this an increasingly likely prospect – the politician who has thought about the implications of coalition politics and knows what he wants will be well ahead of the pack.

15

The Steel strategy

When Steel ended the Lib-Lab pact in September 1978, he expected a general election to come swiftly. In that election, he planned to sing out loud and clear the case for consensus politics. He would point to the benefits which the Lib-Lab pact had brought, such as falling inflation and interest rates and a start to constructive Liberal policies – for example, lower direct taxes and more industrial participation. In the event, the election did not come until six months later.

Some Liberal strategists felt this would be of benefit to the party. In fact, shorn of its direct influence on the government, the Liberals slipped out of the centre stage of politics and lost many opportunities to put their views across. The argument that the party should have time to 'distance' itself from the Labour party before an election proved not to be as sound as had seemed when, in the darkest days of the pact, the Liberals had been taking a lot of stick from the Tory press for keeping Labour in power.

Steel wanted an election as soon as possible. He could see no special benefit in putting the election off until 1979, and did not believe the Liberals would do any better then than they would immediately. Many active workers in the Liberal party were greatly relieved that the pact had ended. Linked as it seemed to them to be with the erosion of votes and support at grass roots level, the pact had caused them nothing but trouble and heartache. Steel viewed it differently. Despite the seeming lack of immediate electoral appeal of pact politics, he still hankered after a brand of coalition politics, and believed the experience of the pact had given the Liberal party greater relevance in British politics. To keep the coalition bandwagon rolling, Steel organised a seminar on coalition governments, which was held in the improbable venue of Berwick-upon-Tweed Town Hall in August. Liberal and radical representatives from Sweden, Norway, Holland, Belgium, Germany and Ireland attended to discuss the kinds of problems which smaller parties encounter when they enter coalitions. The speech which Steel made when he opened the seminar took his thinking on coalition politics several stages further, although he acknowledged mistakes made in the Lib-Lab pact. The speech is important because it can be interpreted as a blueprint for the way in which Steel would approach a coalition in the future.

Steel highlighted three main areas where he wanted further to develop Liberal thinking on coalition-making. The first of these was how long it should take to form a coalition after an election. 'I have always considered it a weakness of the Lib-Lab agreement that, faced with the deadline of a vote of confidence, we had only the limited time from Monday evening to a cabinet meeting on Wednesday morning to construct the agreement,' he said. 'That would be an impossibly short time for an attempt to settle the policy for a full parliament, but fortunately after an election there will be no such tight deadline of forty-eight hours, nor should there be.'

Steel's second area of concern was the arrangements for endorsing partnership proposals in political parties. 'I thought it a drawback of our Lib-Lab agreement that there was no time to secure endorsement by the government party. Thus, when it came to the free vote on the system of election for the European Parliament, a fair chunk of the parliamentary Labour party felt in no way bound by the spirit of the agreement entered into by their leaders. In my view, any form of parliamentary agreement in future must start with the clear endorsement of a majority of the Commons, otherwise frustration like that will recur.'

Thirdly, Steel was concerned about the machinery for maintaining a harmonious partnership between the partners of a coalition. 'Here in Britain, the creation of a Lib-Lab consultative committee was crucial to our agreement. But in practice it dealt mainly with matters of important detail rather than principle. On major issues it tended to get by-passed, in favour of Privy Council terms discussions between the Prime Minister and myself.

'This was almost bound to happen when the arrangement was one not of coalition but of parliamentary partnership outside government. It poses the question of whether minority participation inside government is preferable. Certainly it would enable more positive input.'

Apart from this power talk between men of government, currently and formerly – a form of discourse which Steel has always found most agreeable – Steel also had to resurrect popular support for the Liberals. By the end of the pact, it was languishing at about 5 per cent in the opinion polls. In a television broadcast in July, Steel told viewers it was more important than ever to vote Liberal. 'We've just had a taste of government by common sense, free of the strident spitefulness of the major party organisations, and it works. We've had a rest from the idiocies of the left, from the divisiveness of the Tories, and what we've had is the sort of government many other successful countries in Europe have enjoyed for years. Government of common sense, not class warfare.'

At the assembly in September in Southport, he faced a shell-shocked party and used the occasion to boost morale. Delegates cheered when he proclaimed, 'Single-party government as we have seen it from Labour and Conservative is bad government. To get good government – of the quality which most of our European partners have – we must throw out our indefensible electoral system. We must give Parliament the power and the information to criticise and control government.' As the cheers ricocheted around the hall, thoughtful Liberals reflected they had come a long way since Steel took over the leadership and addressed his first party assembly two years earlier at Llandudno. Then, when he had made a similar statement in his speech, defiant Young Liberals had launched a protest against him.

Despite the taunts from the Tory press that the Liberals, like turkeys, would never vote for an early Christmas, Steel sincerely wanted an early general election. He knew that the economy would deteriorate sharply during the coming winter, and this would hand Thatcher a ready-made bludgeon with which to beat the Labour government, and by implication the Liberals, who had for so long kept it in power. In particular, Steel believed that inflation would worsen sharply in the face of the government's failure to get TUC agreement to a fresh stage of an incomes policy. Denis Healey's 5 per cent had been sharply rejected by the unions.

'The Government is in danger of throwing away the economic stability gained during the period of the Lib-Lab pact,' Steel told Liberal students in November. 'Public opinion is more solidly behind an effective pay policy than are the parliamentary Labour party or the Tory party. And so the government funks bringing in the necessary legislation to create such a policy. It relies on a rigid and troublesome 5 per cent guideline which it attempts to enforce by a series of arbitrary sanctions. Such a policy can last for a short crisis period, as could a total freeze, but it is totally inadequate in the long term.' Steel argued for a long-term incomes policy with three main components.

Firstly, he wanted income increases related to growth in productivity and profitability 'in sections of the economy where this is appropriate'. In Steel's view, this meant extending profit-sharing proposals, which had been a feature of the Lib-Lab pact. 'Any effective incomes policy must start by encouraging local bargaining which relates pay increases to this,' he said.

Secondly, Steel wanted the government, after consultation with bodies like the CBI, TUC and Chambers of Commerce, to lay down the income increase the nation could afford outside productivity schemes. The Liberal way of enforcing this was by a surcharge on the national insurance contributions of any employer who exceeded it – an idea originally dreamed up by Liberal economics spokesman John Pardoe and warmly applauded by some serious journals, such as *The Economist*.

Thirdly, Steel demanded a 'national referee' to act as a pay body to which special cases could be referred. 'It is no good having a series of unrelated inquiries set up into the pay of whoever is threatening strike action. Each government has abolished whatever body its predecessors set up. We need a permanently accepted body of authority, independence and expertise, if a pay policy is to work effectively.'

As the new year dawned, there was still no sign that Labour would lose its perilous hold in Parliament – largely because the minority parties had yet to find an issue around which they could unite to defeat the government. There was also little to suggest that Liberal support was creeping any higher than during the Lib-Lab pact – a fact which depressed many party activists. At the end of January, Steel went on television again to appeal to the nation. His theme was an up-beat version of what he had been peddling since becoming leader.

He said, 'There is urgent need to bring about the rule of law and common sense in our economic life. Yet history shows that no one party can do it on its own. The Conservative government tried and ended in disaster in 1974. The Labour government has tried and is now cracking up with inflation out of control. No one party based on a minority of support from a section of the electorate can cope with this. It needs a united effort. Mrs Thatcher has now offered support to the government tackling our crisis. Good. Let's build on that.'

Steel proposed that the three party leaders should try to reach agreement to discuss the economic and industrial crisis which Britain faced. He said the party leaders should try to reach agreement on two main issues – how pay increases should be decided and the state of industrial relations. 'At these talks we should discuss how to encourage private firms to create and share with their workers as much profit as they can, under agreed rules. We should also discuss the creation of a permanent national referee body for public employees where the claims of special cases and the plight of the lowest paid could be judged impartially.'

He added, 'In the field of industrial relations we must set the limits of lawful industrial action. This might be done by a new industrial relations charter. This would define a new status for employees. It would limit the uses of picketing, it would encourage the greater use of secret ballots before strikes, and deal with the question of the closed shop.' Steel wanted a free vote on these bills because he anticipated wide cross-party support with only a minority of extremists on each side dissenting. To the fury of the other party leaders, Steel invited viewers who agreed with him to write to Callaghan or Thatcher. In the next few days thousands of letters flooded into their offices, and Liberal support leapt a crucial few percentage points in the opinion polls.

As the general election inevitably approached through the spring of 1979, the Liberal party shuddered at the possibility of a major electoral reverse. The opinion polls certainly augured disaster. Liberal voting intentions hovered around 5 per cent – the lowest for years – and a level of support which translated into a general election would effectively decimate the parliamentary Liberal party. The spectre of 1970 haunted Steel. In that year, the parliamentary Liberal party had been reduced from thirteen seats to six as the nation swung to the Tories after a period of unsuccessful Labour government.

However, Steel had some solid reasons for believing he could avert such a disaster this time. The period of the Lib-Lab pact, although it had brought the Liberal party electoral unpopularity, had at least brought it political relevance. Steel believed this would encourage political commentators and the voters to treat the Liberals as a serious political force at the coming election. Further, Steel believed that realignment politics – which he had preached from his earliest days as a political candidate – might at last feature as a central issue in political debate. In Liberal constituencies, MPs could hold their seats by picking up extra votes from Labour, even if they lost some votes to the Tories. In marginal Tory seats, where Liberals were the major challenger, Labour voters might swing behind Steel's men in a drive to get the Tories out. There was already some slender evidence to suggest this might happen. In a by-election in Saffron Walden during the days of the pact, Liberal candidate Andrew Phillips had held his vote reasonably steady by attracting extra support from Labour to compensate for that lost to the Conservatives. And local election results in Liberal-held seats indicated a strong intention to vote Liberal where the party had a realistic chance of electoral success.

Moreover, the Liberals were also in a position to help determine when the government fell as a result of losing a key Commons confidence vote. Steel had consistently maintained since the autumn that no good would be served by the government staggering on from day to day through the winter without a firm Commons majority. So when the Conservatives tabled a confidence motion on 22 March, Steel issued a terse statement: 'In the event of a no-confidence debate, we shall vote for a general election, consistent with our view expressed last autumn.'

In the confidence debate, Steel developed his argument. 'Everything that has happened since October adds weight to the case for fixed-term Parliaments, as in most of the other developed democracies. General election date speculation is one of the few growth occupations in Britain today, absorbing politicians, journalists and bookmakers, but far more seriously, disrupting industry and commerce. That process is damaging and the case has been increasingly made out for moving to a fixed-term Parliament rather than leaving the decision in the hands of one individual.' Steel reiterated that the Liberals' current low standing in the opinion polls was no reason for not having an election. 'Fear of any possible political outcome of a general election is not grounds for allowing the present state of affairs to continue.'

When Steel made the speech, he had good reason for believing that Liberal support would leap in the opinion polls. The day after the confidence vote a crucial by-election took place in the Edge Hill division of Liverpool. Local councillor and community campaigner David Alton seized the seat for the Liberals with a stunning 8,000 majority. Steel could hardly have stage-managed the start of the campaign for the Liberals better. Liberal support in the opinion polls immediately doubled from 5 to 10 per cent – and for the first time for three years it looked as though Steel's strategy might stand a chance of success.

This was Steel's first general election campaign as party leader and he determined to fight it his way – with his strategy. That included the planning of details of the campaign down to the use of a 'battlebus', which the Liberals proudly proclaimed had been hired at a fraction of the cost of the aircraft the other party leaders were using. The vehicle, hired from Park's of Hamilton in Lanarkshire, was an executive coach adapted with a special lounge for the leader, and equipped with radio telephone, two television sets, electric typewriter, photocopier and a coffee machine. Steel, who had thought up the idea for the battlebus, planned to use it visiting the far-flung Liberal strongholds throughout Britain. Press men who wanted to tag along paid £50 a day for a seat.

Steel had decided that he would spend most of the campaign touring Liberal seats, and Tory-held marginals where Liberals had a chance of winning if they could persuade Labour voters to switch their votes to get the Tory out. During a tour of his own constituency the previous autumn, Steel had concluded that his own 7,000 majority was safe, so that he could afford to spend time away from home base.

Steel kicked off the Liberal campaign at a press conference in the National Liberal Club on 9 April. He bluntly told the press, 'We have changed our strategy. In 1974 we claimed we wanted a Liberal government or nothing. In 1979 we are saying something different to the country.' Steel said he wanted a Liberal government in the long run, but in the short term he wanted a 'powerful wedge' of Liberal MPs in the next House of Commons. This would do two things, he said.

'We can stop either main party having things all its own way for five years, imposing their arrogant ideas on us all without having to listen to public opinion. The other thing we can do is to change our system of government so that we begin to look to building co-operation and partnership, without which long-term progress is impossible.' Steel summed up his objectives for the Liberals at the election as a massive Liberal vote everywhere – 'to send them a message they can't ignore' – and many more Liberal MPs in the seats the Liberals had prepared for victory, like Liverpool's Edge Hill, where David Alton had just won a famous by-election victory. 'There can be many more Edge Hills and each one will be a nail in the coffin of confrontation politics,' he declared.

Two problems hung over Steel's campaign – apart, that is, from the concern at every general election that a miniscule swing could, through the vagaries of the first-past-the-post electoral system, wipe out the Liberals as a parliamentary force. (At an eve-of-dissolution dinner in the Commons, the fourteen Liberal MPs faced press reports that only two of their number would return, and they themselves thought half of them might lose.) The first problem was the shadow of violence which hung over the campaign. A few days before Parliament had been dissolved, Airey Neave, shadow Secretary of State for Northern Ireland, and one of Mrs Thatcher's closest confidants, had been brutally blown up by a bomb planted in his car at the House of Commons. As a result, the Home Secretary had warned all political candidates to be on their guard during the campaign – and this particularly applied to the politically prominent, such as the party leaders.

Steel had been allocated a squad of Special Branch detectives to guard him round the clock during the campaign. Steel does not regard himself as a prime target for political extremists, yet in the violent atmosphere the precaution was necessary. The detectives, who had been carefully chosen to fit into the free-wheeling informality of a typical Liberal campaign, became good friends of the campaign staff on the coach. But it is always difficult to be completely friendly with a gun tucked under your jacket. In fact, as one close Steel aide says, the detectives proved helpful during the campaign. When the battlebus visited unfamiliar territory, they would arrange for the local police to meet it at the correct motorway turn off and guide it into town. As the aide recalls, this proved much more reliable than handing the guide job to local Liberals, who would invariably turn up at the wrong motorway junction.

On one occasion, the efforts of the police to protect Steel proved over-zealous. Arriving at Berwick-on-Tweed station late one night to catch the night sleeper back to London, Steel found the train's passengers in dressing gowns and pyjamas grumbling on the platform. An over-efficient police inspector had received a coded message that a VIP was due to travel on the sleeper, and had turned everyone out to search it thoroughly. Steel and his aides slunk quietly aboard, hoping no one would notice them – the political consequences could have been dreadful!

The other problem which haunted Liberal strategists was referred to tersely as the 'Thorpe problem'. Former leader Jeremy Thorpe was due to stand trial at the Old Bailey on charges of conspiracy to murder and incitement to murder. Originally, Thorpe's trial had been due to start just five days before polling day. His lawyers had managed to postpone this until the week after the election. Thorpe had insisted on contesting his North Devon constituency. Although he had meticulously refrained from commenting in public on Thorpe's decision, it was an open secret that Steel strongly disapproved of this. In the lawyers' language of the time, it was felt that Thorpe should dispose of the charges against him before once again mounting the hustings. Steel urged Thorpe privately not to stand.

Steel says, 'My feelings by this time were those of despair. I thought that he had got his whole life into a frightful mess and was unable to extricate himself from it. I think he made a number of decisions which were wrong – fighting that election was one of them.'

However, Thorpe's constituency party strongly backed him, and made it clear they would have no candidate other than Thorpe himself. This left Steel with a delicate tactical problem. Should he visit North Devon during his tour of the Liberal bastions in the West Country? Or should he stay away?

Thorpe had no doubt about his view. He would have welcomed Steel to his seat. Tory newspapers, eager to exploit Liberal difficulties, urged Steel to make a courtesy call on his

174

former leader. But throughout, Steel's view never wavered. He made a notable effort to distance himself from Thorpe as the crisis mounted, and felt strongly that Thorpe should have resigned from Parliament when the criminal charges were brought against him. He had no intention of handing the Tory press, by now in full hue and cry for a Thatcher victory, an easy opportunity to run a smear-by-association campaign if he visited Thorpe. However, a point-blank refusal to aid Thorpe in his hour of need was seen in the Steel camp as being potentially equally damaging.

The problem was finally tackled with a patchy and rather unsatisfactory compromise. Steel sent Thorpe a tape-recorded message of support which could be played at his adoption meeting. Steel announced that he would not be visiting North Devon during the campaign. The reason: there was no time to fit it into a crowded schedule. In fact, when the votes were counted, Liberal strategists could not fault Steel's decision. Thorpe was trounced by his Tory opponent, and the only Liberal MP to support him by making a personal appearance during the campaign, John Pardoe, from the neighbouring North Cornwall constituency, was also defeated. West Country Liberals blamed Pardoe's defeat on a spill-over effect from the Thorpe affair in North Devon.

Steel drove himself remorselessly through a strenuous campaign. A typical day – Wednesday, 25 April – shows just how hard. He kicked off with a press conference at the National Liberal Club in London at 10.20 a.m. Then he dashed by car to Battersea Heliport and flew by helicopter to central Wales. He visited Newtown, Montgomeryshire, in the heart of colleague Emlyn Hooson's constituency, for filmed interviews with BBC Wales and Harlech Television. Then he flew on to Aberystwyth, to give a boost to the campaign of Geraint Howells in his Cardiganshire constituency. After this, the Steel party swung northwards for constituency engagements in Colwyn Bay and Holyhead. Then, at a quarter past four in the afternoon, Steel took another flight to Leeds, followed by a dash by police car, at breakneck speed, complete with sirens and flashing lights, to the Yorkshire Television studio, for a live interview in the *Calendar* magazine programme. The day was still not finished – after the interview he pressed on to a Liberal rally in a Leeds cinema to deliver a major speech on Liberal ideology.

Steel's journeys around the country – with the publicity they attracted – had their effect. The Liberal standing in the opinion polls, which at the beginning of the campaign had been languishing at a dangerously low 5 per cent, climbed steadily. By the last weekend of the campaign most polls predicted that the Liberals could poll nationally 12 per cent or more of the vote. Steel reckoned that if his strategy paid off, and this vote was concentrated in the Liberals' best constituencies, he could return to the Commons with a larger band of MPs than the fourteen who left it. However, there could be no certainty about this – in 1970 a slight decline in the Liberal vote had more than halved the size of the parliamentary party.

Besides, back in Steel's Roxburgh, Selkirk and Peebles constituency, the natives were restless. Steel's party workers reported that they were not too happy with the way in which the campaign had been going. Traditionally, the Borders has been a constituency which likes to see its candidates in the flesh. And although Steel had appeared on the television practically every night of the campaign, the dour Scots who make up his electorate had not been able to shake him by the hand and whisper their little words of encouragement personally. While Steel was away, his wife, Judy, and Lord Mackie, a long-time political friend, toured the constituency on his behalf as surrogate campaigners. The local Tories, who landed an active candidate for the campaign, strongly fancied their chances of unseating Steel.

During the last weekend of the campaign, Steel's agent, Riddle Dumble, strongly urged Steel to scrap the rest of his national tour and spend the remaining time defending his home base. It was a powerful appeal from a man who knows the Borders constituency better than anyone else – perhaps even Steel. Aide Archie Kirkwood clearly recalls the agony which this decision caused Steel. He remembers Steel making up his mind while travelling between two constituency engagements in the battlebus. Steel finally decided to continue with his national campaign at the expense of his constituency. As is usually the case with Steel, the decision was based on clear logical train of reasoning rather than a hunch. He was sure he would win in Roxburgh – but he was not certain that most other Liberal MPs would be returned. His national efforts in the last days of the campaign could just push some of them over the top to victory. In

176

other words, the choice was between a lower majority and a larger parliamentary party, or a higher majority and a smaller parliamentary party. Steel had no doubt which he wanted.

In his last party political broadcast – rated one of the most effective of the election – Steel summed up the nub of his campaign message. Speaking straight to camera, while his son Rory played with a toy car in the background – a ploy designed to remind voters that Steel is a young, family man – he rammed home his theme of co-operation politics. 'There are good people and good ideas in both the other parties, but the party system prevents them ever co-operating. And the good people and good ideas have to give way to the extremists on both sides.'

Steel told his audience, 'I believe that victory for either Tory or Labour in this election will be a defeat for Britain because I believe it will lead increasingly to divisiveness. I believe it's very important not to let either of these groups have things all their own way. One more up or down of the political seesaw will do absolutely nothing to arrest our record of decline.'

The election result, a sweeping win for the Conservatives, did not advance Steel's hope for a radical realignment of political forces or create a situation where Liberals would hold a dominating position in Parliament. With a comfortable majority, Mrs Thatcher could look forward to up to five years in power, without having to worry too much about by-election losses. However, Steel's campaign had been a reasonable success. In the similar circumstances of the 1970 general election, the parliamentary Liberal party was all but wiped out, but this time the party managed to cling on to eleven of its fourteen seats, many of them with increased majorities. Liberal support had risen consistently throughout the campaign reaching 14 per cent of the popular vote on polling day – just 4 per cent lower than the excellent result in October 1974. This was a far cry from the widespread predictions of disaster for the Liberal party which it had suffered in the year or two before, and a qualified vindication of Steel's strategy.

In his own constituency, party managers' fears that Steel's majority might drop proved groundless. His own margin of victory soared to more than 10,000, the largest he had ever enjoyed. He had the added pleasure of polling the largest majority of the three main party leaders.

However, the result meant that Steel's long-term objectives to give the Liberals a position of real power in Parliament had receded. On the face of it, there did not seem to be much chance of that position improving for at least five years. But Steel could look forward to an expected Liberal revival during the mid-term unpopularity of the Tory government.

16

The private Steel

It is not unknown for successful politicians to suffer from an occupational disease known as the walking-on-water syndrome. The politician who suffers from this sometimes terminal condition displays the symptoms of overbearing arrogance and an unshakeable belief that he can do anything. The House of Commons doctor has yet to find a cure for sufferers, who can be spotted by their staring eyes and inability to stop talking.

Fortunately, Steel does not suffer from this distressing condition, although, at the beginning of the 1980s, he can reasonably be counted as one of Britain's most successful politicians. At an age – the early forties – when many men are making their first tentative steps up the ladder of politics, Steel has already reached the top of his party. And although he has not held public office, he did achieve the next best thing – influence over the government of the day during the Lib-Lab pact. In the sixteen years he has been in Parliament, he has moved with sure-footed skill. Even decisions which at the time seemed wrong – like the failure to extract tougher terms as the Liberals' price of entering the Lib-Lab pact – have often been vindicated by later events. As a *Times* leader put it: 'Mr Steel's handling of his party at national level has been consistently impressive.'

In fact, Steel is a shrewd political tactician. He has a fairly rare ability among politicians to be able to see with a reasonable degree of objectivity the likely results of his decisions. This is a necessary precondition of being able to take sound political decisions. He is not invariably right, but in politics it is only necessary to be right more often than you are wrong, in order to be successful. And, as we have seen, Steel learns political lessons quickly, so that he never makes the same mistake twice.

Despite this success, Steel remains very much a quiet family man. Without doubt, the greatest regret of his life is having to spend so much time away from his young family. He has never had what most young marrieds in Britain would call a normal family life. He was already a prospective Liberal parliamentary candidate when he married Judy. A great deal of their time was spent together campaigning, struggling to build up the Liberal vote in Edinburgh Pentlands and then, with great success, in Roxburgh, Selkirk and Peebles. Steel had already been an MP for more than a year when his first child, Graeme, was born. All Steel's children are used to having a father they see only at weekends and during the all too brief parliamentary recesses. As the years roll by, Steel has become even more aware of the missed family life. He is now far more likely to dig in his heels and insist to his staff that they avoid official appointments which clash with family birthdays or special occasions.

He has a running battle with the party over the pressure to attend weekend meetings and conferences and complains that they are insufficently aware of the need to protect what is left of his family life. He will often turn up at party events with one of his children in tow for the weekend. Almost the only Sunday he will appear in London is the annual Remembrance Sunday, and even for that he tentatively suggested that he should not go every year but be represented by somebody else at the Cenotaph. He was dissuaded from this course on the grounds that it would cause unfavourable comment and publicity.

When Steel stood for leader, he astonished some party members by making it clear that, if elected, he planned to carry on living in Ettrick Bridge. He would not become one of the ranks of London-based MPs who only manage to spare their constituencies one weekend a month. In any event, Steel has the kind of constituency where the voters would not take any too kindly to that kind of treatment. The Borders voters like to feel that their MP is one of them, and in Steel they have an MP who *is* one of them.

Steel has lived in Ettrick Bridge now since 1966, and has no plans to leave. Cherrydene, the family home, stands at the end of the one street in Ettrick Bridge, in a gentle hollow. Around it are beautiful green fields. There is a small, attractive garden, obviously not as well kept as it used to be, and a two-car garage. The house itself has a pleasant relaxed feel to it, and is filled with valued possessions collected over the years. Wood fires burn in each of the main rooms, including Steel's study, a book-lined sanctum stuffed with souvenirs of a political career, including, for a Liberal, the obligatory picture of Gladstone, and some admission tickets to Gladstone's Midlothian campaign meetings. When at home, Steel will work here, either at a small desk, or sitting in an armchair by the fire, with his papers scattered over the floor around him. The phone is constantly ringing with messages from his London office, his local agent, or from constituents who want help or advice. Steel's phone number — unlike that of many MPs — is not ex-directory. The number is listed in the phone book, for Steel feels that it is important that he should be accessible to his constituents at all times. When he wants a few hours' peace, he can switch the phone through to the home of two helpers, Archie and Rosemary Kirkwood, who live just a hundred yards down the village street. Archie Kirkwood was Steel's former aide at the House of Commons, and Rosemary was the national organiser for the Young Liberals. Now she helps Steel with some of his local secretarial work.

When Parliament is sitting, Steel usually tries to get back to his constituency by Friday morning. Most of Friday and Saturday are taken up with constituency business, but Sunday remains a day of rest. Steel is an elder of his local kirk. Although he is not now a regular attender, he goes whenever possible. At the weekend, Steel might tinker with his two vintage cars, a 1936 Austin Seven and a 1960 Alvis convertible. He enjoys overhauling them, and takes them to local shows. Steel's interest in the oily mysteries of car engines started at university, when he did his own maintenance on an old banger — the only way he could afford to run a car on a student's vacation earnings. For relaxation, Steel also likes horse riding, or he may take his black Labrador dog, Jill, for a ramble over the local countryside, perhaps shooting rough for the pot.

David and Judy Steel are quite devoted to each other, although their friends are amazed at how different their respective characters are. He is quiet, tough, slightly shy, and disciplined. She is vivacious, bubbling, out-going and somewhat chaotic. It is a case of opposites attracting, for the two are deeply happy, even though political life puts great pressure on their marriage. As in most households, there are strains and stresses, but these are weathered because the Steel marriage is built on solid foundations of mutual love and respect.

There are now four children in the Steel family – Graeme (fifteen), Catriona (thirteen) Rory (eight) and adopted son, Billy (eighteen). It is typical of their generosity and Liberalism that they should have brought Billy into their house as a foster child at the difficult age of thirteen, when his fostering arrangement in a neighbouring home ended. According to friends, this did place a strain on the harmony of the household for a time, a fact which the Steels readily admit, though they believe the experience to have been a rewarding one. Billy is now at drama college in London, having shown considerable natural talent in this field.

All the Steel children attended the local primary school and went on to the state secondary school, although the Steels are not opposed in principle to private education. Indeed, Catriona has just switched to her father's old school, George Watson's in Edinburgh. Both David and Judy have realised that life can be difficult for the child of a famous person in an ordinary state school, but they have decided that it is better to keep the family together than to send the children off to boarding schools.

David and Judy enjoy getting involved in the life of the community as much as possible. They cheerfully turn out for a dance in the village hall and mix perfectly naturally with other villagers. They take special joy in the 'common ridings' festivals which abound in the Borders. Horse riding and swimming are about the only sports in which Steel actually participates.

Family holidays nowadays are taken abroad, usually with one or two of the children in rota, and the Steels spend a weekend holiday each year without the children at the home of their close friends Hille and Nadir Dinshaw in Jersey. The Dinshaws' daughter Nali worked as a secretary in Steel's office, and he is godfather to her daughter Kitty.

During parliamentary sessions, Steel lives in a small flat on the Victoria Embankment in Pimlico. It is only in recent years that Steel has been able to afford this London base. When he first became an MP, he spent his London nights at the National Liberal Club, and then lived for about four years in a basement flat at the Lambeth home of his old university friend Michael Shea, now the Queen's Press Secretary.

Steel is an owl rather than a lark, and during parliamentary sessions his day will start at about eight o'clock. He has a cup of coffee but no breakfast, and listens to the radio news. Sometimes he will take a swim in a nearby pool, but these early morning dips have become less frequent since he became leader of the party. An aide comes at about 9.45 a.m. to take him to the House of Commons by car. Steel spends most of the day at the Commons working in a tiny two-room office suite. He has a small staff of two assistants and two secretaries, whom he drives as hard as himself. None of them complains.

David Steel always chooses his staff carefully. They tend to be young and to be selected less on paper qualifications than on personality. He likes an informal and congenial team around him, to the extent that on one occasion he passed over several eager Liberals for a card-carrying member of the Labour party, on condition only that the membership be allowed to lapse. As an employer, Steel is slow to criticise, but he is also slow to praise.

Since becoming leader of the Liberal party, Steel has been inundated with invitations to lunch and dinner from people who want to meet him. He has only time to attend a fraction of them. He finds lunch with journalists and broadcasters useful, and also occasionally lunches with businessmen or trade unionists. Most weeks, he sets aside some time to meet friends, many of them first made at university, perhaps over a quiet dinner. Steel likes his food, although he eats sensibly. He has wide tastes. He will cheerfully tuck into smoked salmon and Tournedos Rossini in one of London's most expensive restaurants, or sausage and mash in a motorway cafe. A meal will often be accompanied by half a bottle of wine or a bottle of Perrier water at lunch time. Being a true Scot, Steel is not averse to a wee dram, and is no stranger to the finer single malts.

The private Steel, relaxing with friends, can be quite different from the rather buttoned-up, earnest politician the public see on their television screen. He is an amusing and entertaining conversationalist, but he will try not to dominate a gathering in an egotistical way, like some eminent men. He can be more amusing in private than in public, when he knows that the nuances of his utterances are not going to be analysed by political commentators and other pundits. But this is not to suggest that Steel behaves like two different people in public and in private. Rather, the public and the private sides of him emphasise different features of the same character.

Steel has a circle of friends outside politics in whose company he totally relaxes. Some of these, like Michael Shea, his solicitor Denbigh Kirkpatrick, his doctor Lindsay Neil and businessman Norman Hackett, have, with their wives, been friends of both the Steels since university days. Others, like the Dinshaws, the de Souzas and Shahs of Nairobi, Lord and Lady Tanlaw in nearby Eskdalemuir, have become friends through politics. The Steels have a wide circle of friends in Denmark, which they visit often. David Steel's oldest friend, from the age of eleven, is Robert O'Meara, now a successful wildlife artist in Nairobi.

Steel enjoys international travel. He is at home in the campus lecture theatres of the United States, or in the presidential residences of African heads of state. Nyere of Tanzania, Moi of Kenya, Kaunda of Zambia, Mugabe of Zimbabwe all know him well and regard him as an understanding ally on Third World issues. Steel also enjoys the anonymity of foreign travel to foreign cities and remote countryside.

In Liberal politics he also has close friends. He gets on well with all his parliamentary colleagues. Indeed, he makes a point of doing so, even when, or especially when, he finds himself in disagreement with any of them. There are none of the personal tensions and antagonisms which existed under his predecessor. Every one of his colleagues has found himself late at night sitting in the leader's room and pouring out his latest political or personal problems to a sympathetic ear.

Steel chairs the weekly party meetings with sometimes inordinate patience, which rarely snaps. But at a meeting early in 1981, when fellow MPs David Alton, Cyril Smith and David Penhaligon were pressing him to take a vote, he rounded on them angrily, saying that if they ever expected to find themselves in cabinet they would have to learn to accept his summing up the feelings of the meeting as he had just done. Next business. He is so rarely ruffled that the surprise effect when he is can be considerable. He can be irritable when under pressure from too many routine chores in too few days or hours.

He makes an effort to keep at least one evening free a week to dine with his colleagues at the Liberal table in the Members' dining room, though even that is less regular than it used to be. He has no particular confidants among his colleagues, though perhaps Lord Mackie and Russell Johnston, the MP for Inverness, know him best from his early Scottish Liberal party days. He also enjoys the company of the young radical MP from Liverpool Edge Hill, David Alton, who is variously described as a 'bad influence' or a 'good influence' on the party leader, depending on the viewpoint of the opinion-giver. Considering that Alton organised 100 per cent support in his constituency for John Pardoe in the leadership election, the mutual respect they now enjoy is remarkable and stems from campaigning together in the victorious Edge Hill by-election in 1979. Alton jokingly describes himself as Steel's 'deputy chauffeur'.

Most of Steel's colleagues note that he is at his liveliest when Jo Grimond is present and poking irreverent fun at his young leader, the kind of banter Steel enjoys.

One more relaxation is Steel's membership of the Other Club, an exclusive dining club founded jointly by Sir Winston Churchill and Lord Birkenhead. It meets every two months or so, at the Savoy. Its members are limited to fifty in number and include Prince Charles, cabinet ministers, most of the former Prime Ministers, top civil servants, diplomats, Palace officials, and academics. Election is by popular choice, and the criterion is being agreeable to dine with, as well as distinction in one's field. There are significant omissions from the ranks of top politicians.

Some people call Steel shy. He is not so much shy as reserved. He is naturally a very private person, for whom it would be abhorrent to wear his heart on his sleeve. He has emotions, and very strong emotions on some subjects, but they are channelled and controlled by a formidable intellect. One gets the impression that Steel would never give away any of his feelings on a subject accidentally, because he was carried away by the emotion of the moment.

Sometimes this means that Steel seems to function rather like a well-oiled political machine. He knows what his strengths and weaknesses are, and he marshals his resources to give the best possible account of himself. One of his strengths is that he can arrange his thoughts on any subject quickly and logically. He is, therefore, able to present a complex case concisely and effectively. This helped him a great deal, for example, in his piloting of the Abortion Act through Parliament. His low-key presentation of the arguments defused much of the more emotive opposition to it. But it probably did not help him during the days of the Lib-Lab pact, when his presentation of the case for the pact seemed, at times, too dry and clinical. What was needed was a little passion to counter the emotional fury whipped up against the pact.

One of his weaknesses is that Steel does not have the kind of zest for glad-handing which has been thought to be an essential prerequisite for a successful political career. He enjoys meeting people when he has the time to get to know them properly, but the handshake and the quick word on the political stomp is a superficial activity and Steel is inclined to dismiss it as such. Sometimes he gives the impression of being rather glacial, and he can hurt people, but does so unwittingly. Steel has developed a thick skin in his political life, but he can still be hurt. Anyone who attacked his motives, or his family or friends would hurt him.

Steel is undeniably impressive on today's most important political medium, television. He has a well-pitched, carefully modulated voice, slightly accented, which is pleasant to listen to. He has good-looking, regular features, important for a medium which magnifies every fault. And he has clear, frank eyes which shine with sincerity. The whole effect is a picture of transparent honesty and genuineness. One feels, watching him, that he really believes in what he is saying.

Steel is also a very fair person. But in the tough world of politics, fairness can be a weakness as well as a strength. He is said to be too charitable in his judgements of other people. In political arguments, he can see the other person's point of view, and this can mean that he does not press home his own point as strongly as possible in a debate. This should not be confused with the single-mindedness with which he pursues his political objectives. Trying to stop Steel getting what he wants in politics is like trying to stop a Sherman tank – only a very large obstacle will do it. The Lib-Lab pact was a big sea-change in his political career in this respect. It showed him how sheer determination can reap political results, and it stopped journalists writing him off as a kind of ineffective Goody Two-Shoes of British politics.

However, hostile newspapers which depict him as a cynical manoeuvrer only interested in political power are well wide of the mark. If he were only interested in political power, it is hardly likely that he would have joined the Liberal party. He briefly considered joining the Labour party while at university, after hearing a speech by Hugh Gaitskell, but rejected the idea because he recognised even then – in the early 1960s – that the Labour party was an incompatible combination of social democrats and Marxists, and therefore not a reliable agent for the kind of changes which Steel wants to see.

Basically, Steel is a curious and fairly rare political animal, a kind of throwback to the sort of nineteenth-century radicalism epitomised by Gladstone. This elevates the care and dignity of the individual into a high political objective to be protected from the power and intrusions of the state. This is why, for example, Steel is so concerned about the role of the police and immigration officials in relation to immigrants. This nineteenth-century radical tradition makes Steel very aware of the importance of individual freedom, which means a great deal to him. It is, some say, part of the Protestant ethic with which Steel is so deeply imbued, and it is another reason why he rejected the Labour party in favour of the Liberals. Steel believes that the Liberal party should try to prevent the dignity and independence of the individual from being submerged by the growing power of the state.

There is, perhaps, an odd paradox about Steel. Although he is certainly a politician of the times, whose star will continue to rise for some years to come, on a personal level he runs counter to many of the trends in modern-day society. He feels a strong sense of duty, at a time when most people prefer to claim rights rather than responsibilities. He wants to elevate the rights of the individual, when most politicians are concerned with enhancing the powers of the state or of corporate bodies of one kind or another. He is prepared to stand up for an unpopular cause, when most people are only too happy to run with the crowd.

Yet it would be wrong to paint Steel as some kind of latter-day Canute, vainly trying to hold back a sea of wickedness. He is certainly unhappy about many of the trends of contemporary society, such as infringements of human dignity and the encroachment of the state, but he believes society can be changed by the democratic process. He believes that Britain needs fundamental constitutional and political reform as a precondition of being able to make the kind of reforms he wants to see – and the kind of Britain Steel wants to see will combine a staunch defence of individual freedom with a proper concern for social justice. It will be a Britain which releases the energies of its people rather than restricting them, and where enterprise is a means to creating a truly compassionate state.

17

What now for Steel and the Liberals?

Where does David Steel go from here? Will he be yet another Liberal leader whose high hopes end in failure? Or, after so many false dawns, is the Liberal party really poised for a breakthrough in the next few years?

There are certainly reasons to suggest that British politics are undergoing a major structural change similar to the one that took place between the two World Wars, when the Labour party replaced the Liberals as the main force on the radical wing of British politics. It is not just that the Conservative party is moving right and the Labour party left, leaving a giant vacuum in the political centre. More fundamentally, Britain's political structure seems now to be altering to reflect – as it has so far failed to do – Britain's changing place in the world. A two-party system, based on a party of capital and a party of labour, is too blunt an instrument to deal with the complex interplay of issues with which modern governments are faced. The result is that complex political issues, like the management of the economy or the creation of a welfare society, are attacked by the two big parties with the bludgeon of out-dated ideology instead of the subtle surgery of new and flexible political ideas.

Disillusion with the Conservative and Labour parties has grown steadily during the last few decades. The proportion of the vote which the two big parties poll has fallen sharply from about 97 per cent of votes cast in the 1955 general election, to around 80 per cent at the 1979 election. The rise of the nationalist parties as well as the Liberal party have contributed to this. But despite some hopeful moments, notably after the Orpington by-election in 1962 and the February 1974 general election, the Liberal party failed to make a breakthrough. In the first place, the party lacked credibility – it simply did not look like a potential government. Secondly, it lacked a coherent political strategy *and* a clear understanding and acceptance in the party as a whole as to how that strategy might be implemented. It is on this second score that Steel has made a major contribution to the party. He has taken Jo Grimond's airy-fairy ideas about radical realignment, turned them into a coherent political strategy, and explained to his party what this means in terms of the way in which the party must operate and what it must do. There has been opposition in the Liberal party to Steel's strategy, and that opposition will continue, but the majority of leading Liberals now accept that it gives the best prospect for progress, and it has certainly made the party's political stance more credible.

The formation of the Social Democratic party has made the role of the democratic centre of British politics a major issue of political debate, whereas before it was only a peripheral issue. It gives the Liberal party the opportunity to play a much more important role on the political stage than it has done for generations. Steel sees this quite clearly, and he appreciates the opportunities now available to the party, but grasping those opportunities is fraught with many dangers, and Steel sees this also. He is as well equipped as any politician in Britain today to grapple with those dangers. He starts with a big plus. He is thoroughly trusted by his own party. Not all of the members agree with him, but they accept that he is not going to trade the Liberal party for a mess of potage. He is also trusted by the Social Democratic party, and especially the 'Gang of Four'. Some of the Gang, such as Roy Jenkins and Bill Rodgers, have criss-crossed Steel's political career for years, and he knows them well. The SDP's leaders have a respect for Steel's political judgement, and they know he will not put his name to an agreement which he does not intend to keep. Equally important, Steel will not negotiate an agreement which he does not think he can sell to his own party.

Steel also brings to this new political position a wealth of experience of what we might call 'third force' politics. Running a political party without experience of government, and with – until now – only the slenderest prospects of government requires skills and tactics not normally present in the two larger parties. It is an experience which the SDP's Gang of Four are only now sampling. Running a third party requires special skills in developing a viable electoral strategy which will ring bells with the voters, motivating members and running an organisation on limited resources.

It is particularly noteworthy that although it is the creation of the SDP which has provided new focus to the role of the centre in British politics, it is Steel who has been most forthright about what the strategy and tactics of the new political centre should be. In the early months, it has been Steel rather than the SDP leaders who has made the running. It has been Steel who has cut through the confusion and uncertainty, and laid out the pathway to an agreement − first, an agreement on policy, then an agreement on election tactics.

In fact, Steel urged Roy Jenkins and others to form a breakaway movement from the Labour party in a series of intermittent private discussions from July 1979 onwards, long before the actual event in the spring of 1981.

The current shake-up in British politics can be traced to Roy Jenkins's now famous Dimbleby lecture, in which he effectively cut himself loose from the mainstream of Labour politics and produced an analysis of Britain's ills uncannily similar to the one that the Liberals have been propounding for at least twenty years. Steel, who has known Jenkins well since the time he steered his Abortion Act through Parliament while Jenkins was Home Secretary, had meetings with him before and after this lecture to discuss the issues it raised. He also talked with a number of other Labour MPs, and one or two Tories as well, who were sympathetic to the views Jenkins put forward in his lecture. In December 1980, he was telling Fred Emery, political correspondent of *The Times*, in a television interview, 'I don't know whether I'm being used as a shoulder to cry on or whether there is something more serious behind it. I think there is something more serious behind it.'

In fact, by the end of 1980, Steel, who is one of the most careful listeners to the Westminster grapevine, was pretty sure that something like the Social Democratic party was on the cards. Steel was discussing with various disillusioned Labour Members whether there was any prospect of their joining the Liberal party, or whether they should form a fourth force in politics. For those Labour Members, the January 1981 special Labour conference at Wembley was a watershed. The conference voted to change radically the method of electing the party leader and deputy leader, downgrading the importance of Labour MPs – who had previously enjoyed the exclusive right to elect the leader – and giving the largest share of the votes in the leadership contest to the trades unions. This was much worse than even the most pessimistic of the Labour moderates had feared. As a result of that conference, the formation of the SDP moved out of the possible into the probable column. One Labour politician actually considered joining the Liberal party. Steel advised him to become a member of the new SDP.

He explains, 'I thought that it would not be the best course for him to join the Liberal party. The reason is that, although the party would benefit from the addition of politicians from the other parties, unless there was an organised group coming over, it seemed to me that the addition of one or two individuals every two or three months – while, of course, helpful in building up the party – would have nothing like the same cataclysmic impact on the wider political scene as an actual breakaway movement from the Labour party and the fringe of the Conservative party,' Steel told the author in an interview. Steel believes that the enormous leap in support demonstrated in opinion polls for a Liberal-SDP alliance in the months immediately after the formation of the SDP bears out this view. Some of these polls showed the Liberal-SDP alliance leading both the Conservative and Labour parties. 'I do not believe that the Liberal party itself would have scored those figures if we had simply added two or three ex-Labour people to our ranks,' Steel maintains.

He is confident that the Social Democrats will succeed in establishing themselves, and welcomes that success. 'You could say I am open to criticism for actually having turned people away from the Liberal party. However, I think the end result is more satisfactory, and as each week passes it is clear that the thinking of the Social Democrats themselves becomes more coherent, more determined than it was when they first started. For example, when they left the Labour party they tended to rush around saying, "We are the true believers, we stand by the Labour party manifesto of the last election and it is the Labour party that has gone off the rails." That I regard as simply part of the necessary rhetoric, but you don't hear anything now about them saying that they stand by the Labour party manifesto. The word "socialism" is going by the board, and variations like "democratic socialism" are going as well.'

Steel notes, 'It is very interesting that in private conversations with them, there are some hang-ups about leaving the party, but these are decreasing.'

By June 1981, the Liberal and Social Democratic parties had produced a joint document entitled 'A Fresh Start for Britain', which set out in general terms the main areas of agreement between the two parties. The document, which had been carefully constructed from drafts produced separately by the Liberals and SDP, ran to just seven paragraphs. These broad policy objectives, which include a demand for proportional representation, a commitment to the EEC and NATO, and a change from Britain's adversarial style of politics, are being filled out by joint policy commissions.

However, Steel believes that it has been comparatively easy to agree on broad policy objectives, but that it will be much more difficult to make a Liberal-SDP alliance work in the country at large. Steel's views on this are constantly developing, but in the summer of 1981 he took the view that, if it were to work well, the alliance must be a close one. It is his belief that although there must be a division of seats between the Liberals and SDP, this is not the total answer: 'The vast majority of people are non-political and we have to keep reminding ourselves of that. These people are only going to be impressed by this alliance if it is a close alliance, not just an agreement of mutual convenience, a sort of non-aggression treaty. In order to have a dynamic effect on the electorate, we have got to be seen to be working closely together and that means that nationally we have to appear on each other's platforms.'

Steel believes that it may be possible in some constituencies for Liberal and SDP members to join together to select candidates. 'At the moment people react in horror at this suggestion, but I intend to go on pursuing it, as it does seem to me an option which may be easier to organise in some places than a straight division of constituencies.'

Steel is most concerned that this proposed alliance should poll its maximum possible vote. He says, 'It is undoubtedly the case that there will be some Social Democrats in the country who will hesitate at voting for a Liberal candidate and there will be some

Liberals who will hesitate at voting for a Social Democrat. So the case for standing on an alliance ticket or coupon is a strong one.'

But what about rogue candidates – either SDP or Liberal – who might stand against official coupon candidates in such an election? Would Steel be prepared to disown a rogue Liberal candidate who stood in opposition to an official alliance candidate? 'I hesitate to contemplate that, but in the last resort that might have to happen in some cases,' Steel says.

A major policy of the Liberal-SDP alliance at the next election will be electoral reform, if Steel has his way. He says, 'We could achieve that without actually forming a government ourselves, because I think there are now enough supporters of electoral reform in the Labour and Conservative parties. If we ram it very hard in an election and came back as a major third force holding the balance, that would be sufficient to secure electoral reform.

'Electoral reform is certainly a major part of a package of constitutional reform. I believe that constitutional reform is not a dry academic subject, but is a necessary part of a campaign to persuade people that the root causes of some of our problems flow from an unsatisfactory, unwritten constitution, and that if we change the political system, we are more likely to succeed in social and economic terms.'

Steel also wants a strong Liberal-SDP policy on industrial partnership. He says, 'I think we somehow have to get a structure of industrial activity which is infinitely more productive and efficient than it has been, and I don't think that can be solved by looking just at investment grants or extending nationalisation or messing about with the traditional solutions which have been offered by Labour and Conservative governments. We need to have as wide an industrial participation and co-operation as possible. This means extending profit-sharing and co-operation, employee shareholding and introducing works councils into industry. I think it is only against a background of that kind of industrial reform that an incomes policy can be successful.'

An incomes policy will be a key feature of Steel's election platform. He says, 'I think that if you are going to counter inflation, a prices and incomes policy is essential.' But why would a Steel prices and incomes policy succeed when others have failed? 'We would be the first party seeking government which actually advocates a prices and incomes policy before coming to

193

power,' he says. 'Every prices and incomes policy that we have had before has been introduced by governments which have persuaded the electorate to vote for them on the basis of not having one. That seems to me a bad starting point.'

It is a strong possibility that a Liberal-SDP alliance could emerge at the next election as a major force, but without an overall majority. What would it do then? How would it decide which of the other parties to support? Steel says, 'My view is that the basis of that decision must be a comparison between our election platform and the proposals of the other parties, with electoral reform being an issue. We would not start off with either an anti-Labour or anti-Conservative prejudice. We would look at our proposals and decide which would be more likely to deliver. It is on that basis that we would conduct the argument.' So Steel has not ruled out possible co-operation with either the Conservative or Labour party.

What of Steel's own future? If the next election does produce a good result for the Liberals, it is probable that Steel will stay on as leader. Otherwise, he would consider standing down – he has said several times that ten years as party leader is long enough. He is keeping his options open. If he did retire, he would be very attracted by a diplomatic post, possibly in the Third World, or by a job in Scotland, possibly consistent with remaining an MP.

There is no obvious contender for Steel's job at the moment, although there is light-hearted discussion around the Liberal MPs' dinner table from time to time about who should be the next leader. Steel could be expected to favour a solid middle-of-the-roader like Alan Beith, currently the parliamentary Liberal party's chief whip.

The parliamentary Liberal party itself is in a more happy and cohesive state than for many years, thanks to Steel's calm and cool stewardship. The rancour of a few years ago, especially between Jeremy Thorpe and Cyril Smith, has evaporated. Smith is still a maverick member of the party from time to time. He has said some rude things about Steel over the years, but Steel treats these charitably. He says, 'Cyril's weakness is that he does have an engaging bluntness that verges on rudeness. I have never taken it as rudeness and I don't think I have ever felt bad-tempered towards him at all. It's never meant maliciously, which is important, but he is just a bit thoughtless and careless with his tongue. He takes the huff easily, and sometimes doesn't think enough before opening his mouth, but that is a failing in many politicians. He has a very valuable streak of north-country radicalism to bring to the party, and that is something of great value.'

And what of his predecessor Jeremy Thorpe? Would Steel welcome a Thorpe comeback on the political stage? 'My view is that time is a great healer. I don't see him being an asset in the current political situation, but that is not to exclude that he might be at some stage in the future.'

It is far too early to make a considered judgement on the political career of David Steel. By the standards of political life, he is still a young man, with potentially as much as a quarter of a century of active politics ahead of him. If his political life were cut short now, the verdict would have to be of a political talent largely unfulfilled. The Abortion Act, the Lib-Lab pact, the rescue of the Liberal party from despair after the dark days of the Thorpe affair are all notable achievements but inadequate testimony to the political talent and flair which Steel undoubtedly possesses. He needs to be tested by the responsibility of government before a true judgement can be made of his political worth. Steel has said under questioning that he would serve under any one of the Gang of Four as Prime Minister in a joint government. David Owen, Parliamentary leader of the Social Democrats, has likewise said he would readily serve under Steel.

The next five years will be the biggest test yet of his political career. If his sound political judgement, campaigning ability, and capacity for incredibly hard work can be used to pull together a lasting alliance between the Liberals and the SDP, and forge that into an election-winning combination, then he could – just could – emerge as a major politician of the last quarter of the twentieth century. Those who are closest to Steel know that he usually gets what he wants.

Steel for Prime Minister? It's not impossible.

Index

196

198